# *Reading Japanese with a Smile*

*Nine Stories from a Japanese Weekly
Magazine for Intermediate Learners*

# Reading Japanese with a Smile

*Nine Stories from a Japanese Weekly Magazine for Intermediate Learners*

TOM GALLY

*Japan & Stuff Press*

With the exception of Chapter 9, which is new to this edition,
this book was first published
by Kodansha International in 1997 under the title
*Strange but True: A True-Life Japanese Reader.*

Cover design by Koichi Kawamura.

Published by Japan & Stuff Press, Mihara 2-19-60-202,
Asaka-shi, Saitama-ken 351-0025, Japan.

Japanese text from "Dekigotology," *Shūkan Asahi.*
Copyright © Asahi Shimbunsha.

ISBN: 978-4-9902848-1-7

First edition by Japan & Stuff Press, September 2007

www.japanandstuff.com

# CONTENTS

# INTRODUCTION

Most Japanese-language textbooks make language learning simple and systematic. They carefully limit the number of kanji introduced at each level. They present new vocabulary and grammatical patterns step by step. Most important of all, they choose topics that are easy for readers to understand and unlikely to offend any teachers or students. The only problem with these textbooks is that they generally are very, very dull.

The boredom induced by textbooks contrasts sharply with the rich and stimulating variety of the Japanese press. Some fifty thousand books are published every year in Japan on subjects ranging from philosophy to pornography. Thousands of magazines clog the racks of bookstores and newsstands, offering entertainment and debate, scandal and libel, the high, the middlebrow, and the very low. It is this world, the world of Japanese as it is really written, into which this book is intended to provide a glimpse.

The nine stories in this book were chosen from the "Dekigotology" column that appeared in the magazine 週刊朝日 *Shūkan Asahi* for many years. The word *dekigotology* (デキゴトロジー) is a combination of 出来事 *dekigoto*, which means "event" or "happening," and the Greek/English suffix *-logy*. Dekigotology, in other words, is the study of things that happen. Each week, the column carried a half dozen stories, all purported to be true, about interesting events that had happened to people recently. The stories generally concern subjects that are familiar or topical, and their interest lies in the way they reveal what happens behind the scenes of everyday life.

The stories are often surprising and usually funny.

The stories on the following pages were selected from the hundreds that ran in "Dekigotology" in the early 1990s. To be chosen, each story had to meet two criteria: it had to be interesting, and it couldn't be so topical that it would quickly go out of date. There was also an attempt to choose a variety of topics.

## Organization

Each story is presented first in its entirety, exactly as in the paperback book edition, with kanji pronunciations marked only when they appeared in the original. An English translation appears on the facing page. This translation is intended to help the reader understand the Japanese, so it is more literal in places than a smooth literary translation would be. Students of Japanese may want to avoid looking at the translation until they have finished reading the text and notes.

Next, the story is presented again a sentence or two at a time, with the reading of every kanji marked with furigana. Each of these text excerpts is followed by several groups of notes.

The first notes, marked with the kanji 語 (short for 語彙 *vocabulary*), consist of short glosses of words and phrases that appear in the preceding sentence. Every word is explained except basic grammatical function words (は, が, を, etc.) and words that have appeared earlier in the same story.

The second group of notes, marked with the kanji 動 (short for 動詞 *verb*), consists of reverse derivations of declined verbs and adjectives. The first word in each derivation is the form that appears in the sentence, while the last word is the form that would normally appear in dictionaries. For example, the series 疑わなかった ☞ 疑わない ☞ 疑う *utagau* goes from the past-tense negative to the nonpast negative to the nonpast affirmative (or dictionary) form of this verb.

The third group, marked with 注 (short for 注釈 *an-

*notation*), consists of detailed notes on the vocabulary and grammar. Special attention is given to identifying the subjects of verbs and to showing which nouns are modified by which adjectives, relative clauses, etc. These notes also include remarks on usage, related words, and typographical conventions, the last being a topic rarely mentioned in Japanese textbooks.

The notes in the final group, marked 文 (short for 文化 *culture*), provide information and commentary about the cultural background of the stories. When necessary, they also explain what makes the stories particularly interesting or funny to the Japanese reader.

Pronunciations are marked in the notes using romaji, not furigana. There are several reasons for this. Furigana are sometimes hard to read, especially when the type is small. Romaji are useful for showing word divisions and identifying the readings of the particles は and へ, such as in the phrase という のは *to iu no wa*. And for students who have learned Japanese from teachers who prohibit the use of romaji, the romaji scattered through the notes will familiarize them with this method of representing Japanese pronunciation, which is still essential for scholars and for others who use both Japanese and English in international contexts.

## Acknowledgments

I am grateful to many people for their help in the preparation of this book. I first learned of "Dekigotology" over two decades ago from Tomoko Iwai, who was one of my Japanese teachers at the time, and her enthusiasm for making language learning interesting as well as educational was one of the inspirations for this book. I am also thankful to Hiroko Fukuda and Kazushi Ishida, who made valuable contributions to an early draft, to Michael Brase and Shigeyoshi Suzuki of Kodansha International for their helpful suggestions during the planning stages and for their careful editing of the first edition in 1997, and again to Michael Brase, now executive director of Japan &

Stuff Press, for offering to publish this expanded edition.

Special gratitude also goes to the *Asahi Shimbun* for kindly granting permission to reprint the stories here and to Shinchosha for permission to use the versions published in book form. Readers who wish to read more of these stories are encouraged to purchase the paperback anthologies in the 朝日文庫 *Asahi Bunko* and 新潮文庫 *Shinchō Bunko* series.

I would also like to thank the participants in the Honyaku mailing list for their wise and informative discussions on many matters related to Japanese and English translation. For their responses to questions I posted about this book, I am particularly indebted to Sara Aoyama, Adrian Boyle, John Brannan, Regina I. A. Brice, John Bryan, John De Hoog, Alan Gleason, Graham Healey, Rich Higgins, Brian Howells, Sako Ikegami, Dan Kanagy, Yosuke Kawachi, J. C. Kelly, Mamoru Kondo, Bill Lise, David J. Littleboy, John Loftus, Tammy J. Morimoto, Gururaj Rao, Adam Rice, Karen Sandness, Fred Uleman, Rodney Webster, and John Zimet.

As always, I am indebted to my wife, Ikuko Gally. She provided many comments and suggestions about each of the stories in this book, and her insights greatly improved the accuracy and depth of the notes.

Although all of these people did their best to help me, I fear that I have betrayed their kindness by persisting in many errors, for each of which I take full responsibility.

Tom Gally

# まえがき

　日本語を学ぶ外国人にとって、最大の悩みの一つは教科書の内容が面白くないということだ。初級レベルでは、基本語彙、日常会話などを修得する必要があるから、仕方がないのかもしれないが、中級以上のテキストになっても、楽しんで読めるものがほとんど載っていない。「日本の経済について」とか「平和を守ろう」という、百科事典や新聞の社説に出るような一般論や建前論、あるいは「スミスさんは靴を買う」のような、役には立つかも知れないが、実際には退屈な話ばかりが載っているからだ。そのような教科書で日本語を勉強すると、日本はつまらない国だ、日本人は感情に乏しい人種だ、といった誤解さえ生じかねない。

　しかし、日本に住み、日本の映画、テレビ、漫画などを見ていると、この国が他の国に負けないぐらい複雑な面を持っているということがわかる。上品で優雅な面もあるし、下品でけばけばしい面もある。

　私は東京で日本語を勉強していたとき、日本語学校で使っていた教科書が嫌になると、よく近くの本屋に行って立ち読みした。まだ日本語がほとんど読めなかった頃でも、そこに並んだ本、特に雑誌の多様性、面白さに強い魅力を感じた。一日も早くそのような生の日本語を読みたかった。上級クラスになると、やっと教科書以外の読み物が使われるようになった。それが「デキゴトロジー」だった。

「デキゴトロジー」が初めて週刊朝日に載ったのは昭和53年頃だった。当初からは、このコラムのポリシーは本当の出来事を面白く伝えることにある。その内容は色々

な分野に渡っているが、私たちが日常経験する恥ずかしいこと、いやらしいこと、ずるいことなどが中心となっている。建前ばかりの教科書を読んでいた私にとっては、クラスで知った「デキゴトロジー」の生々しい人間性が新鮮な空気のようだった。今でも「デキゴトロジー」を紹介してくださった岩井智子先生に感謝している。

　以上の理由で、この本を作った。平成に入ってからの話を九つ選んで、翻訳と詳細な注釈を付けた。対象読者は日本語を学習する外国人だが、日本のことを英語でどういうふうに説明するか、または外国人の目で日本語や日本人はどのように見えるか、ということに興味のある日本人にも読んでいただければ大変嬉しい。

# 嫁のデキ心で知る
# 有名スーパーの誠意

## THE HONESTY OF A FAMOUS SUPERMARKET, REVEALED BY A DAUGHTER-IN-LAW'S SUDDEN URGE

# 嫁のデキ心で知る
# 有名スーパーの誠意

世田谷のS子さん（三一）宅に、逗子に住む姑、F子さん（六一）が訪ねてきたのは、梅雨の晴れ間の昼のことだった。

「渋谷まで来たから、ちょっと孫の顔を見にね」

S子さんにとっては鬼より怖い姑である。精いっぱい愛想よくもてなした後、娘を連れて散歩にいってもらった。

ホッと一息。気が緩んだせいか、空腹を覚えたS子さん、ふと、姑が近くの高級スーパー「Kノ国屋」で買ったというドーナツの袋に目が止まった。逗子の自宅用といっていたから、

（これには手を出せないわね）

と一度は思ったものの、空腹は理性より強し。袋を開けると、中には六個のドーナツ。

# THE HONESTY OF A FAMOUS SUPERMARKET, REVEALED BY A DAUGHTER-IN-LAW'S SUDDEN URGE

It was midday during a dry spell in the rainy season when F-ko (61) came from Zushi to visit the home of her daughter-in-law S-ko (31) in Setagaya.

"Since I had already come as far as Shibuya, I just dropped by to see my grandchild's face."

For S-ko, her mother-in-law was more frightening than a demon. S-ko did everything she could to be a good hostess for F-ko. Later, her mother-in-law took S-ko's daughter for a walk.

S-ko breathed a sigh of relief. As she relaxed, S-ko felt hungry, and her eyes suddenly came to rest upon the bag of doughnuts that her mother-in-law had bought at K-nokuniya, a luxury supermarket nearby. F-ko had said that she was going to take the doughnuts home to Zushi.

S-ko thought at first, "I really shouldn't touch them."

But hunger is stronger than reason. She opened the bag and found six doughnuts inside.

（一個だけなら分からないか）

　と、急いで食べると、パックの蓋を念入りに元に戻しておいた。そうとは知らぬ姑は、散歩から戻ると、ドーナツの袋を提げて、満足げに帰っていった。

　ところが、逗子に戻ったＦ子さん、しっかり、一個足りないのに気がついたから大変。

「天下のＫノ国屋がこんなミスをするなんて！」

　と、さっそくＫノ国屋に延々三十分の抗議の電話。Ｋノ国屋の担当者も根負けした。翌朝一番に、八十円のドーナツ一個を後生大事に抱え、販売員と売り場の責任者がＦ子さん宅まで謝罪にきたのである。片道二時間余り。聞けば、販売員はそのため五時に家を出たという。

　Ｆ子さんもこれには、

「さすがにＫノ国屋だわー」

　と大感激。友人やＳ子さんに吹聴して回った。もちろん、それを聞いたＳ子さんは、顔面蒼白。この秘密は、墓場まで持って行こうと固く決心している。

"Maybe she won't notice if I eat only one," S-ko thought. She hurriedly ate a doughnut and carefully re-closed the package.

F-ko returned from her walk none the wiser. Quite satisfied with herself, she left for home carrying the bag of doughnuts.

But sure enough, when F-ko returned to Zushi, she noticed that one doughnut was missing. That's when the trouble started.

"I can't believe that, of all the stores in Japan, K-nokuniya would make such a mistake!" F-ko immediately called K-nokuniya to complain. The call dragged on for thirty minutes. F-ko was too much for the person handling the matter at K-nokuniya. The first thing the next morning, clutching a single 80-yen doughnut as if their lives depended on it, the sales clerk and the floor supervisor came to F-ko's home to apologize. One way, it had taken more than two hours. When asked, the sales clerk said she had left home at five o'clock that morning.

F-ko was greatly impressed. "That's K-nokuniya for you!" she said.

She spread the story around to her friends and S-ko. Of course, when S-ko heard what had happened, her face turned deathly pale. She has firmly resolved to take the secret to her grave.

## COMMENTARY

### 1a

*Title:* 嫁のデキ心で知る有名スーパーの誠意

語　嫁 *yome* daughter-in-law / デキ心 *dekigokoro* (bad) impulse / で知る *de shiru* to find out from; to be shown by / 有名 *yūmei* famous / スーパー supermarket / 誠意 *seii* honesty; sincerity

注　デキ心 is usually written 出来心. Katakana is often substituted for kanji or hiragana in informal writing as a kind of playful emphasis. / The phrases 嫁のデキ心で知る and 有名スーパーの both modify 誠意.

### 1b

世田谷のS子さん（三一）宅に、逗子に住む姑、F子さん（六一）が訪ねてきたのは、梅雨の晴れ間の昼のことだった。

語　世田谷 *Setagaya* residential area in western Tokyo / S子さん *Esu-ko-san* Ms. S., S-ko / 三一 ☞ 三十一歳 *sanjū-issai* 31 years old / 宅 *taku* home, residence / 逗子 *Zushi* city near Kamakura, about 50 km south of central Tokyo / 姑 *shūtome* mother-in-law / 訪ねてきた *tazunete kita* came to visit / 梅雨 *tsuyu* the rainy season, which usually comes to all of Japan except Hokkaido in June / 晴れ間 *harema* a brief dry spell

動 訪ねて ☞ 訪ねる *tazuneru* / きた ☞ 来る *kuru*

注 The word 宅 can come immediately after a person's name without a connecting の, so Ｓ子さん宅 means "S-ko's home." / The phrase 逗子に住む姑 modifies Ｆ子さん, so 逗子に住む姑、Ｆ子さん means "F-ko, (S-ko's) mother-in-law, who lives in Zushi." / The topic of this sentence is Ｆ子さんが訪ねてきたのは "(the time when) F-ko came to visit"; the の is a nominalizing particle. This topic is linked by the copula だった to 梅雨の晴れ間の昼のこと. The core meaning of the sentence is thus "the time when F-ko came to visit was around midday during a brief dry spell in the rainy season."

文 The principal characters in the "Dekigotology" stories, and in many similar articles in the popular press, are identified by their initials. The 子 in Ｓ子 marks it as a woman's name, perhaps 幸子 *Sachiko* or 静子 *Shizuko*. The mother-in-law Ｆ子 might be 文子 *Fumiko* or 藤子 *Fujiko*. Not all women's names end in 子, however, and sometimes you may see names like Ｈ美 (for 春美 *Harumi*) or Ａ奈 (for 安奈 *Anna*). / The ages 三一 and 六一 are written in kanji here because that is how they appeared in the original vertically-printed article. In horizontal Japanese text, the numbers would normally be written as 31 and 61. / The kanji 姑 is not one of the 1,945 characters of the 常用漢字 *jōyō kanji* list recommended by the Japanese government for general use. Aside from school textbooks and newspapers, few publications adhere rigorously to that list, and the student of Japanese who learns only the 常用漢字 will remain incompletely literate.

## 1c

「渋谷まで来たから、ちょっと孫の顔を見にね」

語 渋谷 *Shibuya* a major business, shopping, and entertainment area on the west side of central Tokyo / 孫 *mago* grandchild / 顔 *kao* face

動 来た ☞ 来る *kuru* / 見 ☞ 見る *miru*

注 What F-ko means to say at the end of this sentence is ちょっと孫の顔を見に来たんです "I just dropped by to see my grandchild's face." F-ko's omission of the verb is a breezy, familiar style that is common in speech and informal writing. The stories in this book contain many verbless sentences. / The symbols 「 and 」 are used here as quotation marks. Called 鈎括弧 *kagi kakko* "key brackets" because of their resemblance to Japanese L-shaped keys (鈎 *kagi*), these marks are also used for emphasis and to indicate proper names, as in 1g and 6j.

## 1d

S子さんにとっては鬼より怖い姑である。

語 S子さんにとっては *Esu-ko-san ni totte wa* for S-ko, in S-ko's opinion / 鬼 *oni* devil; demon / 怖い *kowai* frightening

注 The topic phrase of this sentence is understood to be F子さんは.

文 Conflicts between married women and their husbands' mothers are a frequent theme of popular fiction and television dramas, reflecting, perhaps, the prevalence of such conflicts in real life.

---

**1e**

精いっぱい愛想よくもてなした後、娘を連れて
散歩にいってもらった。

---

語 　精いっぱい *sei ippai* as much as possible, with a total effort / 愛想よく *aiso yoku* cheerfully; warmly / もてなした entertained (her) / 後 *ato* after / 娘 *musume* daughter / 連れて *tsurete* taking along / 散歩に *sanpo ni* for a walk / いってもらった had gone; [lit.] received (her) going

動 　もてなした ☞ もてなす / 連れて ☞ 連れる *tsureru* / いって ☞ 行く *iku* / もらった ☞ もらう

注 　The subject of もてなした and もらった is Ｓ子さん, and the subject of 連れて and いって is Ｆ子さん.

文 　The image of a daughter-in-law playing the perfect hostess while secretly fearing her mother-in-law would be familiar to many Japanese readers.

---

**1f**

ホッと一息。

---

語 　ホッと with relief / 一息 *hitoiki* a short rest; [lit.] one breath

注 　As in 1a, the katakana in ホッと indicate a mild emphasis, similar to italic type in English. This word appears in dictionaries as ほっと. / Again the verb is omitted. The full idiom is 一息つく *hitoiki tsuku* "to take a breather."

---

**1g**

気が緩んだせいか、空腹を覚えたＳ子さん、ふと、姑が近くの高級スーパー「Ｋノ国屋」で買ったというドーナツの袋に目が止まった。

語　気が緩んだ *ki ga yurunda* relaxed; became less tense, less vigilant; [lit.] the 気 *ki* became slack / せい because / 空腹 *kūfuku* empty stomach; hunger / 覚えた *oboeta* felt / ふと suddenly / 近くの *chikaku no* nearby / 高級 *kōkyū* high-class; luxury / 「Ｋノ国屋」 *Kēnokuniya* abbreviated name of supermarket / 買った *katta* purchased / という *to iu, to yū* which (F-ko) said (she bought) / ドーナツの袋 *dōnatsu no fukuro* bag of doughnuts / 目が止まった *me ga tomatta* (S-ko) noticed; [lit.] (S-ko's) eye stopped on

動　緩んだ ☞ 緩む *yurumu* / 覚えた ☞ 覚える *oboeru* / 買った ☞ 買う *kau* / 止まった ☞ 止まる *tomaru*

注　The phrase 気が緩んだせいか means "perhaps because she relaxed," explaining why S-ko suddenly felt hungry. / The topic-marker は *wa* after S-ko-san has been elided. / While 覚える often means "to remember" or "to learn," here its meaning is "to feel." / 姑 is the subject of 買った. / Ｓ子さん is the topic for 目が止まった.

文　Tokyo residents would recognize Ｋノ国屋 as 紀ノ国屋 *Kinokuniya*, a luxury supermarket that sells imported food. (There's also an international chain of bookstores called Kinokuniya, but they write their name 紀伊國屋.)

---

**1h**

逗子の自宅用といっていたから、（これには手を
出せないわね）と一度は思ったものの、空腹は
理性より強し。

---

語　自宅用 *jitaku-yō* for use at one's home / といっていた
から *to itte ita kara* because (F-ko) had said that / 手を出
せない *te o dasenai* cannot touch; cannot get involved in
/ わね (shows mild exclamation; used by female speakers)
/ ものの *mono no* but / 空腹は理性より強し *kūfuku
wa risei yori tsuyoshi* hunger is stronger than reason

動　いって ☞ 言う *iu* or *yū* / いた ☞ いる / 出せない ☞
出せる ☞ 出す *dasu* / 思った ☞ 思う *omou*

注　The kanji 用 is used as a suffix in many expressions similar to 自宅用. Examples include 客用 *kyakuyō* "for use
by guests," 軍用 *gun'yō* "for military use," and 社用 *shayō*
"for company use." / The parentheses in （これには手を
出せないわね） and in 1j indicate S-ko's unspoken
thoughts. / 強し is the archaic literary form of the adjective 強い *tsuyoi* "strong." / F子さん is understood to be
the subject of いっていた, while S子さん is the subject
of 出せない and 思った.

文　The phrase 空腹は理性より強し is a pun on the pro-
verb ペンは剣より強し *pen wa ken yori tsuyoshi* "The pen
is mightier than the sword."

---

## 1i

袋を開けると、中には六個のドーナツ。

語 開けると *akeru to* when (S-ko) opened / 中には *naka ni wa* inside / 六個 *rokko* six (roundish objects)

注 In full, this sentence would end 六個のドーナツがあった.

## 1j

（一個だけなら分からないか）と、急いで食べると、パックの蓋を念入りに元に戻しておいた。

語 一個だけなら *ikko dake nara* if only one (doughnut is missing) / 急いで食べる *isoide taberu* to eat in a hurry / パック package / 蓋 *futa* cover / 念入りに *nen'iri ni* carefully, meticulously / 元に戻しておいた *moto ni modoshite oita* reclosed (the package); [lit.] returned (the cover) to its original position (in preparation for F-ko's return)

動 分からない ☞ 分かる *wakaru* / 急いで ☞ 急ぐ *isogu* / 戻して ☞ 戻す *modosu* / おいた ☞ おく

注 The particle と is used in two distinct meanings in this sentence. The first と can be called the "quoting" と; it is used to report speech, names, or, in this case, thoughts. The quoting と often appears with the verb 言う "to say" or 思う "to think"; it is also used in 1g and 1h, for example. The second と is the "sequential" と; it shows that one action follows another. Examples of the sequential と appear in 1i and 1k.

文　S-ko's impulsive doughnut eating is the デキ心 mentioned in the story's title.

---

**1k**

そうとは知らぬ姑は、散歩から戻ると、ドーナツの袋を提げて、満足げに帰っていった。

---

語　そうとは知らぬ姑 *sō to wa shiranu shūtome* her mother-in-law, who didn't know about that / 散歩から戻ると *sanpo kara modoru to* when (she) returned from her walk / 提げて *sagete* carrying / 満足げに *manzokuge ni* with a satisfied look / 帰っていった *kaette itta* went home

動　知らぬ ☞ 知る *shiru* / 提げて ☞ 提げる *sageru* / 帰って ☞ 帰る *kaeru* / いった ☞ 行く *iku*

注　The ぬ ending on 知らぬ is a more literary version of the negative suffix ない; 知らぬ has the same meaning as 知らない. / The basic meaning of the verb 提げる is "to dangle; to let hang." When the object is a shopping bag, handbag, or other object with a strap or handle, the verb is best translated as "to carry."

---

**11**

ところが、逗子に戻ったＦ子さん、しっかり、一個足りないのに気がついたから大変。

---

語　ところが however (i.e., contrary to what was expected or hoped) / 戻った *modotta* returned / しっかり surely; without missing a thing / 足りない *tarinai* to be lacking; to be missing / 気がついた *ki ga tsuita* noticed / から because / 大変 *taihen* a major crisis

動　戻った ☞ 戻る *modoru* / 足りない ☞ 足りる *tariru* / ついた ☞ つく

注　The adverb しっかり, which modifies 気がついた, suggests that F-ko is the type who lets very little get past her. / As in 1b, the particle の is a nominalizer, so 一個足りないの means "(the fact) that one doughnut was missing." / Note that the meaning of から depends on the form of the verb it follows. After the past or present tense, it means "because": 気がついたから "because she noticed." When preceded by the gerund (*-te*) form, however, it means "after": 気がついてから "after she noticed." / The word 大変 often expresses shock or panic. Someone who finds that the bathtub has overflowed and soaked the tatami is likely to shout 「大変だ！」 "Oh, no!" The word's use in the above sentence expresses S-ko's sense of impending disaster. / The copula だ after 大変 has been elided.

**1m**

「天下のＫノ国屋がこんなミスをするなんて！」
と、さっそくＫノ国屋に延々三十分の抗議の電話。

語　天下の *tenka no* unsurpassed; leading / こんなミス such
a mistake / なんて (expresses doubt, surprise, or anger) /
さっそく immediately / 延々 *en-en* at length; longwind-
edly / 抗議 *kōgi* complaint / 電話 *denwa* telephone call

注　As the kanji suggest, the original meaning of 天下 is
"under heaven," that is, "the entire country" or "the
world." When used as a modifer, 天下の means "widely
known to be the best." / The traditional pronunciation of
十分 in the meaning "ten minutes" is *jippun*, not *juppun*
as shown above. While the former pronunciation can be
heard in news broadcasts and the like, the latter is more
common in contemporary speech. (When 十分 means
"enough; sufficient," it is pronounced *jūbun*.) / With the
unstated verb added, this sentence would end ...抗議の電
話をした.

**1n**

Ｋノ国屋の担当者も根負けした。

語　担当者 *tantō-sha* the person handling the matter / 根負け
した *konmake shita* gave up

動　根負けした ☞ 根負けする *konmake suru*

注　根負けする means "to give up because one's opponent is
more persistent."

**1o**

翌朝一番に、八十円のドーナツ一個を後生大
事に抱え、販売員と売り場の責任者がＦ子さん
宅まで謝罪にきたのである。

語　翌朝一番 *yokuasa* (or *yokuchō*) *ichiban* the first thing the next morning / 八十円のドーナツ一個 *hachijū-en no dōnatsu ikko* one 80-yen doughnut / 後生大事に *goshō daiji ni* with infinite care / 抱え *kakae* holding (his or her arms around) / 販売員 *hanbai-in* sales clerk / 売り場 *uriba* sales floor (of the supermarket) / 責任者 *sekinin-sha* the manager; the person with senior responsibility / 謝罪に *shazai ni* to apologize

動　抱え ☞ 抱える *kakaeru* / きた ☞ 来る *kuru*

注　Other combinations with 翌 include 翌日 *yokujitsu* "the next day" and 翌週 *yokushū* "the next week." / 抱え is the stem of 抱えます *kakaemasu*, the present formal of 抱える. The present formal stem is used to link clauses. / The difference between 謝罪にきたのである and just 謝罪にきた is that the の followed by the copula である indicates that this sentence is an elaboration of the preceding sentence: it explains what happened after the 担当者 gave up in the face of F-ko's complaints.

文　The term 後生 is so close in form and meaning to the English "afterlife" that one might think it a loanword. In fact, though, 後生大事 comes from Buddhism and originally meant "caring more about the next life than about this one." In this story, the meaning is more secular. The supermarket employees were worried about not the Great Beyond but the store's reputation. There's a bit of sarcasm, too, in the use of this full-powered 漢語 *kango* to describe how someone carried an eighty-yen doughnut.

---

**1p**

<ruby>片<rt>かた</rt>道<rt>みち</rt></ruby>二<ruby>時<rt>じ</rt></ruby>間<ruby>余<rt>あま</rt></ruby>り。<ruby>聞<rt>き</rt></ruby>けば、<ruby>販売員<rt>はんばいいん</rt></ruby>はそのため<ruby>五<rt>ご</rt>時<rt>じ</rt></ruby>に<ruby>家<rt>いえ</rt></ruby>を<ruby>出<rt>で</rt></ruby>たという。

---

**語** 片道 *katamichi* one-way (trip) / 二時間余り *ni-jikan amari* over two hours / 聞けば *kikeba* when (F-ko) asked / そのため for that purpose / 五時に *goji ni* at five o'clock / 家を出た *ie o deta* left home

**動** 聞けば ☞ 聞く *kiku* / 出た ☞ 出る *deru*

**注** The opposite of 片道 is 往復 *ōfuku* "round trip." / Other expressions with 片 include 片手で *katate de* "with one hand" and 片方 *katahō* "one (of a pair)." / After a numerical expression, 余り means "somewhat more than," as in 十人余り *jūnin amari* "more than ten people; a dozen or so people." / In this sentence, そのため means "in order to make the one-way trip of over two hours." / The unstated subject of 聞けば is F子.

**文** Nowhere is the gender of the 販売員 specified, nor that of the 担当者 or the 売り場の責任者. Each could be either male or female. This ambiguity is often impossible to maintain in translations into English, in which gender-specific pronouns are unavoidable.

## 1q

F子さんもこれには、「さすがにＫノ国屋だわー」と大感激。

語 さすがに really; as expected / 大感激 *daikangeki* greatly moved; deeply touched

注 これ "this" refers to the long journey made by the supermarket employees. / The vowel of the exclamation particle わ is lengthened to わー *wā* as emotive emphasis. / 大 *dai* is a prefix meaning "greatly; very much." / The particle と here is the quoting と (see 1j). / The verb of this sentence is 感激した *kangeki shita*, with the した omitted.

## 1r

友人やＳ子さんに吹聴して回った。

語 友人 *yūjin* friends; acquaintances / 吹聴して回った *fuichō shite mawatta* proclaimed; spread the word

動 回った ☞ 回る *mawaru*

注 By itself, 吹聴する means "to announce; to spread (news) widely." The 回った emphasizes that F-ko told this story to one person after another.

## 1s

もちろん、それを聞いたＳ子さんは、顔面蒼白。

語　もちろん of course / 顔面 *ganmen* face / 蒼白 *sōhaku* pale; pallid

動　聞いた ☞ 聞く *kiku*

注　With the omitted verb replaced, the sentence would end 顔面蒼白になった "her face blanched."

文　The kanji 蒼 in 蒼白 means "blue" or "green." It also has the kun reading *ao*.

## 1t

この秘密は、墓場まで持って行こうと固く決心している。

語　秘密 *himitsu* secret / 墓場 *hakaba* grave / 持って行こうと *motte ikō to* to carry away / 固く *kataku* firmly; resolutely / 決心している *kesshin shite iru* has decided; has resolved

動　持って ☞ 持つ *motsu* / 行こう ☞ 行く *iku*

文　S-ko's determination to carry to the grave the secret of her furtive doughnut eating has two motives. One is her embarrassment at having forced the supermarket employees to take such a long journey for the sake of an 80-yen doughnut. The other motive, which gives a sharper edge to this story, is S-ko's continuing fear of what her mother-in-law would do if she ever found out.

# 2

亡き友担いで登った
富士山頂の初日の出

*A New Year's Dawn on the Summit of Mt. Fuji, Climbed While Carrying a Dead Friend*

# ❷ 亡き友担いで登った
## 富士山頂の初日の出

東京で編集者をしているＴさん（三三）は年末、郷里の静岡の友人と元旦の富士登山を約束した。ところが、大晦日に電話すると、友人は交通事故を起こし危篤だという。病院に駆けつけたらすでに亡くなっていた。

ひとしきり号泣した父親は、Ｔさんに哀願した。

「私も一緒に富士山に登ることになっていた。どうかこれから息子を登らしてやってくれ！」

そばにいた婦長も感動して、

「私もついていきますから」

という。そして二人はＴさんを連れ出し、本当に遺体を車に乗せ、富士山に向かったのである。

途中、年末警戒の検問に遭った。警官は車内を覗き込み、

「そちらの方、顔色が悪いですね」

# A New Year's Dawn on the Summit of Mt. Fuji, Climbed While Carrying a Dead Friend

T (33), who works as an editor in Tokyo, had promised to climb Mt. Fuji on the morning of New Year's Day together with a friend from his native area, Shizuoka. But when T telephoned him on New Year's Eve, he was told that his friend had been in a traffic accident and was near death. T rushed to the hospital only to find that his friend was already dead.

Having sobbed for a while, his friend's father appealed to T: "I was supposed to go along to climb Mt. Fuji. Please do something so that my son can climb it now!"

The head nurse, who was nearby, was moved by this and said, "I'll go along, too."

So the father and nurse led T outside, and they actually did put the dead body in the car and head for Mt. Fuji.

Along the way, they were stopped for questioning as part of the year-end safe-driving campaign. A police officer peered into the car and said, "That fellow looks sick."

と聞く。間もなく遺体であることがバレたが、事情を知った警官は感動してパトカーで先導してくれた。

婦長を麓に残し、三人が大沢登山道を登り始めたのは夜の十時。遺体をおぶったのは重量挙げをやっていたTさんである。気温は氷点下十五度。すでに死後硬直が始まり、Tさんは何度も転び、血だらけになった。

午前五時半、やっと頂上に辿り着いた。焚き火をたくと、友人の体が少し温かくなった。

「生き返ったんじゃないか」

と、父がひとりつぶやいた。

七時少し前、いきなり朝日が差した。友人を挟み、Tさんも父も涙が止まらなくなった。

あれから五年が過ぎた。二月に友人の父から突然、便りが届き、中に自動シャッターで撮った三人の写真が同封されていた。友人は笑っているように見える。父は、フィルムを現像に回すまで五年かかったのである。

Tさんは、また涙が止まらなくなった。

Soon the fact came out that it was a corpse. When he understood the situation, the officer was so moved that he led the way for them in his patrol car.

Leaving the head nurse at the foot of the mountain, the three began to ascend the Osawa Trail. The time was ten o'clock at night. T, who used to lift weights, carried the body piggyback. The temperature was fifteen degrees below zero Celsius. Rigor mortis had already begun to set in, and T fell down several times and got covered with blood.

At half past five in the morning, they finally reached the summit. They built a fire, and the body of T's friend warmed up a little.

"It looks like he's come back to life," the father muttered to himself.

Just before seven, the morning sun suddenly shone on them. As they sat on either side of T's friend, neither T nor the father could stop crying.

Five years have passed since then. In February, a letter arrived unexpectedly from the friend's father. Enclosed was a photograph of the three of them, taken with a self-timer. The friend seemed to be smiling. It had taken the father five years to send the film to be developed.

Once again, T couldn't stop crying.

## COMMENTARY

**2a**

*Title:* 亡き友担いで登った富士山頂の初日の出

語 亡き友 *nakitomo* dead friend / 担いで *katsuide* carrying on one's shoulders / 登った *nobotta* climbed / 富士山頂 *Fuji-san-chō* the summit of Mt. Fuji / 初日の出 *hatsuhinode* the first sunrise of the year

動 担いで ☞ 担ぐ *katsugu* / 登った ☞ 登る *noboru*

注 The verb 登った modifies 富士山頂 and 亡き友 is the object of 担いで, so 亡き友担いで登った富士山頂 means "the summit of Mt. Fuji, climbed while carrying a dead friend on one's shoulders." / The prefix 亡き *naki* "dead" is also used in other combinations, such as 亡き人 *nakihito* "deceased person" and 亡き父 *nakichichi* "one's late father." / The prefix 初 *hatsu* means "the first of the year," as in 初湯 *hatsuyu* "one's first bath of the New Year" and 初詣 *hatsumōde* "New Year's visit to a shrine."

文 One of the many customs associated with the New Year's season in Japan is viewing the first sunrise of the New Year. People go to mountaintops and east-facing seashores on the morning of January 1 to see and photograph the year's first dawn. Because of the cold and snow, though, only the most intrepid attempt to climb Mt. Fuji, which at 3,776 meters (12,388 feet) is the highest peak in Japan.

**2b**

東京で編集者をしているＴさん（三三）は
年末、郷里の静岡の友人と元旦の富士登山を
約束した。

語　東京で *Tōkyō de* in Tokyo / 編集者 *henshū-sha* editor /
年末 *nenmatsu* at the end of the year / 郷里 *kyōri* home
town; native area / 静岡 *Shizuoka* name of a prefecture
and city southwest of Tokyo / 友人 *yūjin* friend / 元旦
*gantan* the morning of New Year's Day / 登山 *tozan*
mountain climbing / 約束した *yakusoku shita* promised

動　して ☞ する / 約束した ☞ 約束する *yakusoku suru*

注　The phrase 東京で編集者をしているＴさん means "T,
who works as an editor in Tokyo." / Series of nouns
linked by の are sometimes difficult to parse. Here 郷里
の静岡の友人 means "a friend from T's native area,
Shizuoka." / 富士登山 is "climbing Mt. Fuji."

文　The "Dekigotology" editors assert that all of the stories in
this series are true. One piece of evidence to support this
claim is the high proportion of characters who are editors, designers, or employees of publishing companies—in
other words, the sort of people who are likely to be acquaintances of the series' writers.

---

**2c**

ところが、大晦日に電話すると、友人は交通
事故を起こし危篤だという。

---

語　ところが however (i.e., contrary to what was expected) /
大晦日 *Ōmisoka* the last day of the year / 電話すると
*denwa suru to* when T telephoned / 交通事故 *kōtsū jiko*
traffic accident / 起こし *okoshi* had caused / 危篤 *kitoku*
close to death

動　起こし ☞ 起こす *okosu*

注　交通事故を起こす means "to be in a traffic accident." /
The と after 電話する is the sequential と, while the と
after 危篤だ is the quoting と (see 1j). / Tさん is the
subject of 電話する, and 友人 is the subject of 起こし
and 危篤だ. / The subject of いう is the unidentified
person who told T of his friend's accident over the telephone.

---

**2d**

病院に駆けつけたらすでに亡くなっていた。

---

語　病院 *byōin* hospital / 駆けつけたら *kaketsuketara* when
(T) hurried (he found that) / すでに already / 亡くなっ
ていた *nakunatte ita* had died

動　駆けつけたら ☞ 駆け付ける *kaketsukeru* / 亡くなって
いた ☞ 亡くなる *nakunaru*, いる

注　駆け付ける means "to rush or hurry to a destination." /

---

The subject of 駆けつけたら is Ｔさん, and the subject of 亡くなっていた is 友人. / Here, the たら suffix suggests that the matter described in the following clause—that is, the death of T's friend—was surprising or unexpected.

> **2e**
>
> ひとしきり号泣した父親は、Ｔさんに哀願した。

語 ひとしきり for a while / 号泣した *gōkyū shita* sobbed; wailed / 父親 *chichioya* father / 哀願した *aigan shita* appealed; begged

動 号泣した ☞ 号泣する *gōkyū suru* / 哀願した ☞ 哀願する *aigan suru*

注 父親 is the subject of both 号泣した and 哀願した. / 父親 is more formal than 父 *chichi*.

---

**2f**

「私も一緒に富士山に登ることになっていた。ど
うかこれから息子を登らしてやってくれ！」

---

語　私も *watashi mo* I also / 一緒に *issho ni* together (with
you and my son) / ことになっていた was supposed to,
was going to / どうか (word used with requests) / これ
から now; soon / 息子 *musuko* my son / 登らしてやっ
てくれ *noborashite yatte kure* let [have] him climb the
mountain (as a favor to me)

動　なっていた ☞ なっている ☞ なる / 登らして ☞ 登ら
す ☞ 登る *noboru* / やって ☞ やる / くれ ☞ くれる

注　The pattern ことになっている follows the plain form
of the verb and means "is supposed to" or "has been decided to." / 登らして is the gerund of 登らす, which is
the literary causative form of the verb 登る. The usual
spoken causative form is 登らせる. / The verb やる here
means "to give," with Ｔさん as the giver of the action
and the father as the recipient. / くれ is the brusque imperative of くれる "to do for me." The brusque imperative is seldom used in formal situations or by women.
The more polite version of くれ is ください.

---

**2g**

そばにいた婦長も感動して、「私もついていき
ますから」という。

---

語　そば nearby; next to / 婦長 *fuchō* head nurse / 感動して

---

*kandō shite* was moved (emotionally) / ついていきます go along with; accompany

動　いた ☞ いる / 感動して ☞ 感動する *kandō suru* / ついて ☞ 付く *tsuku* / いきます ☞ 行く *iku*

注　そばにいた婦長 means "the head nurse, who was nearby." / The 婦 of 婦長 is the same as the last character of 看護婦 *kangofu* "nurse." / The sentence 私もついていきますから literally means "Because I'll go with you, too." The explanatory から "because" indicates that the head nurse is giving another reason why T should take his friend's body to Mt. Fuji—because she will accompany them.

---

## 2h

そして二人はＴさんを連れ出し、本当に遺体を車に乗せ、富士山に向かったのである。

---

語　そして then; next / 二人 *futari* the two people (i.e., the father and the head nurse) / 連れ出し *tsuredashi* led (T) outside / 本当に *hontō ni* actually / 遺体 *itai* corpse; body / 車 *kuruma* car / 乗せ *nose* placed (into the vehicle) / 富士山に向かった *Fuji-san ni mukatta* headed for Mt. Fuji

動　連れ出し ☞ 連れ出す *tsuredasu* / 乗せ ☞ 乗せる *noseru* / 向かった ☞ 向かう *mukau*

注　乗せる is the transitive counterpart of 乗る *noru* "to ride; to get in a vehicle." / 連れ出し and 乗せ are the stems of the present formal forms 連れ出します and 乗せます, respectively. As in 2j, 2l, and 2o, these stems link clauses. / The sense of 本当に in this sentence is "actually went so far as to (put the corpse into the car)."

---

**2i**

途中、年末警戒の検問に遭った。

語 途中 *tochū* along the way / 年末警戒 *nenmatsu keikai* year-end safety [safe-driving] campaign / 検問 *kenmon* inspection; questioning / 遭った *atta* encountered; came across

動 遭った ☞ 遭う *au*

注 遭う is one of several ways to write the verb あう. When the meaning is "to meet; to rendezvous with," the word is written 会う. The meaning "to match; to align" is written 合う. When written 遭う, the verb means "to encounter by chance; to happen to meet." 遭う is usually used of unfortunate experiences.

文 During 年末警戒, the police do spot checks on passing vehicles, looking for drunk drivers, undone seatbelts, and other traffic violations. In this case, they may also have been hoping to turn back some of the motorcycles and cars packed with young people that gather at the base of Mt. Fuji for a raucous celebration of the New Year.

**2j**

警官は車内を覗き込み、「そちらの方、顔色が悪いですね」と聞く。

語 警官 *keikan* police officer / 車内 *shanai* interior of vehicle / 覗き込み *nozokikomi* peeked into / そちらの方

*sochira no kata* that person / 顔色が悪い *kaoiro ga warui* looks sick / 聞く *kiku* ask; inquire

動 覗き込み ☞ 覗き込む *nozokikomu*

注 The verb 覗き込む "to peek into" is a compound of 覗く *nozoku* "to peek" and 込む *komu* "to put into." / そちらの方 is the polite version of その人 *sono hito* "that person." / The idiom 顔色が悪い literally means "his facial color is bad," but "looks sick" is closer to the intended meaning. / The verb 聞く indicates that the police officer spoke in a questioning tone. As suggested by the sentence-final ね, he was asking for confirmation that T's friend really was sick.

---

**2k**

間もなく遺体であることがバレたが、事情を知った警官は感動してパトカーで先導してくれた。

語 間もなく *ma mo naku* soon / 遺体であること *itai de aru koto* the fact that it was a corpse / バレた was revealed / 事情 *jijō* the situation / 知った *shitta* learned; found out / パトカー patrol car / 先導してくれた *sendō shite kureta* led the way (for T and the others)

動 バレた ☞ ばれる / 知った ☞ 知る *shiru* / 先導して ☞ 先導する *sendō suru* / くれた ☞ くれる

注 The idiom 間もなく literally means "without even an interval of time," in other words, "very soon." / The verb ばれる is used when lies, conspiracies, or other secrets are discovered. / 事情を知った警官 means "the police officer, when he found out about the situation."

---

---

**21**

婦長を麓に残し、三人が大沢登山道を登り始めたのは夜の十時。

---

語　麓 *fumoto* the foot of the mountain / 残し *nokoshi* leaving behind / 三人 *sannin* the three people / 大沢登山道 *Ōsawa Tozandō* the Osawa Trail / 登り始めたのは *nobori-hajimeta no wa* when they began climbing / 夜の十時 *yoru no jūji* ten o'clock at night

動　残し ☞ 残す *nokosu* / 登り始めた ☞ 登る *noboru*, 始める *hajimeru*

注　三人 is the subject of 残し and 登り始めた.

文　Is it surprising that 三人 "three people" should refer to two living people and a corpse? This may reflect the traditional Japanese belief that some portion of the soul of a dead person continues to inhabit the physical remains. This would also explain why T and the father decided to carry the corpse up the mountain in the first place.

---

**2m**

遺体をおぶったのは重量挙げをやっていたTさんである。

---

語　おぶった carried on his back / 重量挙げ *jūryō-age* weight lifting / やっていた had done; used to do

動　おぶった ☞ 負ぶう *obuu* / やって ☞ やる / いた ☞ いる

---

注　The verb 負ぶう means "to carry on one's back." / 遺体をおぶったのは means "the one who carried the dead body"; this phrase is linked by the copula である to 重量挙げをやっていたTさん "T, who used to do weight lifting."

---

### 2n

気温は氷点下十五度。

語　気温 *kion* air temperature / 氷点下 *hyōtenka* below the freezing point / 十五度 *jūgo-do* fifteen degrees (Celsius)

注　−15°C is +5°F.

---

### 2o

すでに死後硬直が始まり、Tさんは何度も転び、血だらけになった。

語　すでに already / 死後硬直 *shigo kōchoku* rigor mortis / 始まり *hajimari* had begun / 何度も *nando mo* several times; again and again / 転び *korobi* fell down / 血だらけ *chi-darake* covered with blood / なった became

動　始まり ☞ 始まる *hajimaru* / 転び ☞ 転ぶ *korobu* / なった ☞ なる

注　The kanji of 死後硬直 show the meaning: "death-after-hard-straight," that is, "stiffening after death" or "rigor mortis." / The verb 転ぶ describes the action of tripping or slipping and then falling down. / The suffix だらけ also appears in 泥だらけ *doro-darake* "covered with mud."

---

---

**2p**

ごぜん ご じ はん　　　　ちょうじょう たど　つ
午前五時半、やっと頂上に辿り着いた。

---

語　午前五時半 *gozen goji-han* half past five in the morning /
やっと finally; at last / 頂上 *chōjō* summit / 辿り着いた
*tadoritsuita* reached

動　辿り着いた ☞ 辿り着く *tadoritsuku*

注　The verb 辿り着く means "to reach a goal after suffering
or hardship."

---

**2q**

たき び　　　　　　　　　ゆうじん　からだ　すこ　あたた
焚き火をたくと、友人の体が少し温かくなった。

---

語　焚き火 *takibi* bonfire / たく light (a fire) / 友人の体
*yūjin no karada* T's friend's body / 少し *sukoshi* a little bit
/ 温かくなった *atatakaku natta* warmed up

動　たく ☞ 焚く *taku* / 温かく ☞ 温かい *atatakai* / なった
☞ なる

注　The adjective あたたかい "warm" is written 温かい
when it means "warm to the touch" or "friendly; cordial"
and 暖かい when it means "warm air temperature."

---

**2r**

「生き返ったんじゃないか」と、父がひとりつぶ
やいた。

語　生き返った *ikikaetta* came back to life / ひとり to himself / つぶやいた muttered

動　生き返った ☞ 生き返る *ikikaeru* / つぶやいた ☞ 呟く
*tsubuyaku*

注　The ん after 生き返った is a spoken form of the explanatory nominalizer の, and じゃない is a contraction
of ではない "not." / The ending じゃないか means
roughly "it looks like (he's come back to life)."

**2s**

七時少し前、いきなり朝日が差した。

語　七時少し前 *shichi-ji sukoshi mae* shortly before seven
o'clock / いきなり suddenly / 朝日 *asahi* the morning
sun / 差した *sashita* shone (upon them)

動　差した ☞ 差す *sasu*

---

**2t**

友人を挟み、Ｔさんも父も涙が止まらなくなった。

語　挟み *hasami* sitting [standing] on either side of / Ｔさんも父も *T-san mo chichi mo* both T and the father / 涙 *namida* tears / 止らなくなった *tomaranaku natta* wouldn't stop

動　挟み ☞ 挟む *hasamu* / 止らなく ☞ 止らない ☞ 止る *tomaru* / なった ☞ なる

注　The verb 挟む means "to place or press between." It is the source of the noun 鋏 *hasami* "scissors." / The compound phrase Ｔさんも父も is the topic of the verb phrase 止らなくなった; the subject is 涙. / A literal translation of Ｔさんも父も涙が止らなくなった might be "Both T's and the father's tears wouldn't stop."

---

**2u**

あれから五年が過ぎた。

語　あれから since then / 五年が過ぎた *gonen ga sugita* five years passed

動　過ぎた ☞ 過ぎる *sugiru*

**2v**

二月に友人の父から突然、便りが届き、中に自動シャッターで撮った三人の写真が同封されていた。

語 二月 *nigatsu* February / 突然 *totsuzen* unexpectedly / 便り *tayori* letter / 届き *todoki* was delivered / 中に *naka ni* inside / 自動シャッター *jidō shattā* self-timer; automatic shutter / 撮った *totta* taken / 三人の写真 *sannin no shashin* a photograph of the three people / 同封されていた *dōfū sarete ita* was enclosed (in the envelope)

動 届き ☞ 届く *todoku* / 撮った ☞ 撮る *toru* / 同封されている ☞ 同封される ☞ 同封する *dōfū suru*

注 The context here suggests that 便り refers to a letter. In other situations, the word can also mean "news (about a person)" or "communication." / 自動シャッターで撮った三人の写真 means "a picture of the three people, taken with a self-timer." The verb 撮った modifies 写真. / When とる "to take" refers to the taking of photographs, videos, etc., it is written 撮る. / 同封する means "to enclose in the same envelope."

---

**2w**

友人は笑っているように見える。

語 笑っている *waratte iru* smiling; laughing / ように見える *yō ni mieru* appears to be; seems to be

動 笑っている ☞ 笑う *warau*

注 笑う can mean either "to smile" or "to laugh." (To keep this story from becoming too macabre, let's suppose that the corpse is only smiling.)

---

**2x**

父は、フィルムを現像に回すまで五年かかったのである。

語 フィルム *firumu* film / 現像に回す *genzō ni mawasu* send for developing / 五年かかった *gonen kakatta* it took five years

動 かかった ☞ かかる

注 As in 1o, the final のである indicates that the preceding clause is an explanation of what came earlier. Here, it explains that the letter from the father came five years later because it took him that long to get up the courage to develop the film.

## 2y

Ｔさんは、また涙が止まらなくなった。

語　また again

注　This sentence is an echo of 2t.

# 3

## 創作日記に秘める
## 女のしたたかさ

### A Woman's Shrewdness
### Concealed in a Fictional Journal

# 創作日記に秘める
# 女のしたたかさ

　都内の商社に勤めるＦ子さん（二五）は、就職活動まっ盛りの大学生、Ｔ君（二三）と同棲中である。今春、

「俺、情けないほど作文に弱いんだ。入社試験の練習に日記を書くから、添削してくれる？」

　と彼に相談され、

「じゃあ、私もつきあって書くわ。でも、ただの日記じゃつまらないから、私のは全部フィクションの嘘つき日記ね」

　と快諾、互いに見せ合うことに決めた。学生時代は作家を夢見たこともあるＦ子さん、毎夜、罪のないフィクションを書き連ねて楽しんでいたが、Ｔ君は大絶賛。

「上手いな、すごく面白い！」

　しかし、彼女、最近になってこの嘘つき日記に新たな楽しみを見いだしてしまった。

# A Woman's Shrewdness
## Concealed in a Fictional Journal

F-ko (25), who works for a trading company in Tokyo, is living with T (23), a college student who is in the midst of looking for a job.

This spring, T asked F-ko, "I'm so bad at writing it's pitiful. I'm going to keep a diary as practice for employment exams. Would you check it for me?"

She readily agreed. "In that case, I'll keep one, too. But a simple diary would be boring, so mine will be all lies, total fiction, okay?"

And so they decided to show each other their diaries. When F-ko was in college, she had sometimes dreamed of becoming a writer, so every evening she had a good time writing out her innocuous fiction.

T thought her writing was great. "You're good," he said. "This is really interesting!"

But recently she found a new way to enjoy her fabricated journal.

「いま、会社に気になる人がいる。彼も私に興味があるみたいで、食事に誘ってくれたり。年下のＴじゃ、結婚は先だし……」

この進行中の浮気を、さりげなく嘘つき日記に書くときの快感がたまらない。

「今日はＴがコンパで遅い。私は会社の彼と、雰囲気のあるバーへ。店を出る際、彼の腕が私の肩にさりげなく回ったときは、新たな恋の予感を感じて……」

これもＦ子さんの"創作"と信じて疑わないＴ君は、

「リアリティーあるよね。ゾクゾクしちゃう」

と無邪気なもの。

「日記のおかげで、彼の行動は全面ガラス張りだし、私の浮気は完全フィクションってことになってるし。しばらく、この交換日記やめられないわ」

したたかに笑うＦ子さんである。

*There's someone at the company who's been on my mind these days. He seems interested in me, too. He invites me out to eat and things like that. After all, T's younger than me and marriage is a long way off....*

She gets an inexpressible thrill as she writes nonchalantly in her fictional journal about her ongoing affair.

*T had a party tonight and was late getting home. I went with the man from the office to a mellow bar. When we came out of the bar, he casually put his arm around my shoulder. I felt the premonition of a new romance....*

Believing without a doubt that this story was also F-ko's invention, T was all innocence. "It's so realistic," he said. "I get all excited."

"Thanks to his diary, I know everything that T does, while my affair is supposed to be completely fictional. I won't be able to give up swapping diaries for a while."

F-ko laughs shrewdly.

## 3a

*Title:* 創作日記に秘める女のしたたかさ
(そうさく にっき ひ おんな)

語　創作 *sōsaku* creative work; imagination / 日記 *nikki* diary; journal / 秘める *himeru* hidden; kept secret / 女の *onna no* a woman's / したたかさ shrewdness; wiliness

注　As the story explains, a 創作日記 is a diary or journal that is supposed to be a work of the imagination. / The word したたかさ is the noun form of the adjectival noun 強か *shitataka* (also written 健か) "shrewd; stubborn; wily." / 女のしたたかさ can mean either "a woman's shrewdness" or "the shrewdness of women." / The verb 秘める modifies したたかさ.

## 3b

都内の商社に勤めるＦ子さん（二五）は、就職活動まっ盛りの大学生、Ｔ君（二三）と同棲中である。

語　都内 *tonai* within Tokyo / 商社 *shōsha* trading company / 勤める *tsutomeru* works; is employed / 就職活動 *shūshoku katsudō* job-hunting / まっ盛りの *massakari no* in the midst of; at the height of / 大学生 *daigaku-sei* university student / Ｔ君 *Tī-kun* Mr. T / 同棲中 *dōsei-chū* now living together

注 The 都 in 都内 is the last character in the official name of Tokyo, 東京都 *Tōkyō-to* "Tokyo Metropolis." / 就職 means "getting a job" and 活動 "activities." / まっ盛り appears in dictionaries as 真っ盛り. / The phrase 就職活動まっ盛りの大学生、T君 means "T, a college student who is in the midst of looking for a job." / The suffix 中 *chū*, as in 同棲中, indicates that something is currently taking place, as in 工事中 *kōji-chū* "under construction," 検討中 *kentō-chū* "under evaluation," and 戦争中 *sensō-chū* "in a state of war."

文 A 商社 is a company whose main business is buying and selling products, commodities, or services. Although the term is often translated as "trading company," many 商社 do business primarily or exclusively within Japan. The large, powerful Japanese trading companies that operate internationally are called 総合商社 *sōgō shōsha*. / The 就職活動 of a typical university student involves requesting information from companies, preparing separate hand-written résumés for each potential employer, visiting companies for tests and interviews, and asking friends, teachers, and relatives for advice and contacts. For most four-year college students, 就職活動 is the culmination of a lifetime of study and determines the student's future career and social standing. / The suffix 君 kun is added after a surname or given name. Usually used in place of さん with the names of boys or men, it indicates that the speaker or writer regards the other person as a friend or subordinate. It is not used when speaking to or about an older person. In this story, it suggests that T, as a university student, is still regarded as young by the writer or readers. / The term 同棲 can mean simply "living in the same home," but, as in this case, it often describes a man and woman living together out of wedlock.

## 3c

今春、「俺、情けないほど作文に弱いんだ。

語　今春 *konshun* this spring / 俺 *ore* I; me (masculine, informal) / 情けないほど *nasakenai hodo* to a pitiful degree / 作文 *sakubun* writing; composition / 弱い *yowai* weak

注　Like 僕 *boku* "I; me," 俺 is used only by men. 俺 is less polite than 僕 and is not used when speaking to superiors or in formal situations. / The particle ほど means roughly "so much that...; to such an extent that...." / The phrase 情けないほど作文に弱い means "so bad at writing that it's pitiful." / The ん in 弱いんだ is a contracted form of the explanatory particle の.

## 3d

入社試験の練習に日記を書くから、添削してくれる？」と彼に相談され、

語　入社試験 *nyūsha shiken* company entrance examination / 練習 *renshū* practice / 日記を書くから *nikki o kaku kara* I'm going to keep a journal, so... / 添削してくれる？ *tensaku shite kureru?* could you correct it for me? / 彼に相談され *kare ni sōdan sare* (F-ko) was consulted by him

動　添削して ☞ 添削する *tensaku suru* / 相談され ☞ 相談される ☞ 相談する *sōdan suru*

注　添削する means to correct or revise another person's writing. / The subject of 書く is 俺 (T君), while the subject of 添削して and 相談され is F子. T wants to practice writing because employment tests often include essay questions.

**3e**

「じゃあ、私もつきあって書くわ。でも、ただの日記じゃつまらないから、私のは全部フィクションの嘘つき日記ね」と快諾、互いに見せ合うことに決めた。

語 じゃあ well, in that case / つきあって書く *tsukiatte kaku* write together with you / わ (shows emotive emphasis; used by female speakers) / でも but / ただの simple; plain; unadorned / じゃ (contraction of では *de wa*) / つまらない boring / 私のは *watashi no wa* mine; my journal / 全部フィクションの *zenbu fikushon no* completely fictional / 嘘つき *usotsuki* lying; false / 快諾 *kaidaku* agreed cheerfully / 互いに *tagai ni* to each other / 見せ合う *miseau* to show (to each other) / こと (nominalizer) / 決めた *kimeta* decided

動 つきあって ☞ 付き合う *tsukiau* / 決めた ☞ 決める *kimeru*

注 付き合う here means "to do something together." / The particle じゃ, from では, indicates the topic of つまらない, so ただの日記じゃつまらない literally means "as for only a diary, that would be boring." / Both フィクション and 嘘つき mean "not true," though フィクション is often used in the sense of literary fiction while 嘘つき refers to a deliberate lie or deception. / The use of the sentence-ending particle ね after a noun or adjectival noun, as in 日記ね, is a feature of women's speech. Men would say 日記だね. / The omitted verb after 快諾 is して, the gerund form of する. / 互いに見せ合うことに決めた means "they decided to show (their journals) to each other." / The subject of 快諾(して) is Ｆ子さん, while the subjects of 見せ合う and 決めた are Ｆ子さん and Ｔ君.

---

**3f**

学生時代は作家を夢見たこともあるＦ子さん、毎夜、罪のないフィクションを書き連ねて楽しんでいたが、Ｔ君は大絶賛。

---

語　学生時代 *gakusei jidai* when (F-ko) was a college student / 作家 *sakka* writer; author / 夢見たこともある *yumemita koto mo aru* had sometimes dreamed about / 毎夜 *maiyo* every night / 罪のない *tsumi no nai* without sin; innocuous; harmless / 書き連ねて *kakitsuranete* writing at length; writing an extended work / 楽しんでいた *tanoshinde ita* was enjoying; was having fun / 大絶賛 *dai zessan* lofty praise

動　夢見た ☞ 夢見る *yumemiru* / 書き連ねて ☞ 書き連ねる *kakitsuraneru* / 楽しんで ☞ 楽しむ *tanoshimu* / いた ☞ いる

注　学生 means "college student"; the word normally does not refer to students of high schools, vocational schools, etc. / 時代 means "era; period of time," so 学生時代 literally means "the period when (F-ko) was a college student." / The clause 作家を夢見たこともある modifies Ｆ子さん, so 作家を夢見たこともあるＦ子さん means "F-ko, who sometimes used to dream of being a writer." The も in こともある here means "sometimes; in addition to other things." / 絶賛 means "high praise"; the prefix 大 adds emphasis. / With the omitted verb added, this sentence would end Ｔ君は大絶賛した.

---

---

**3g**

「上手いな、すごく面白い！」

語　上手い *umai* skillfully done / な (indicates appreciation) / すごく very / 面白い *omoshiroi* interesting; fun

注　Without the okurigana い, 上手い becomes the adjectival noun 上手 *jōzu*, which means "skillful; talented." / すごく is the adverbial form of 凄い *sugoi* "frightening; terrifying; amazing; extreme." The use of すごく to mean "very," though common in speech, is discouraged by some conservative grammarians.

---

**3h**

しかし、彼女、最近になってこの嘘つき日記に新たな楽しみを見いだしてしまった。

語　しかし however / 彼女 *kanojo* she / 最近になって *saikin ni natte* recently / 新たな *arata na* new / 楽しみ *tanoshimi* enjoyment / 見いだしてしまった *miidashite shimatta* discovered

動　見いだして ☞ 見いだす *miidasu* / しまった ☞ しまう

注　最近になって is nearly the same as 最近 *saikin*, which also means "recently," but 最近になって emphasizes a change in situation. Here, it shows that F-ko has just discovered a new kind of enjoyment. / The gerund (*-te*) form followed by しまう indicates that the action of the verb has unfortunate consequences. In the case of 見いだしてしまった, the pattern is used ironically, as the conse-

---

quences are unfortunate for T, not for F-ko. (In other contexts, the gerund + しまう form may indicate merely that the action of the verb is completed.)

---

**3i**

「いま、会社に気になる人がいる。彼も私に興味があるみたいで、食事に誘ってくれたり。年下のＴじゃ、結婚は先だし……」

---

語　いま now / 会社 *kaisha* (my) company; (my) office / 気になる人 *ki ni naru hito* a person I'm thinking about / 彼 *kare* he / 興味があるみたい *kyōmi ga aru mitai* seems to be interested / 食事 *shokuji* meals / 誘ってくれたり *sasotte kuretari* invites me (to meals) (and other things) / 年下 *toshishita* younger (than me) / 結婚 *kekkon* marriage / 先 *saki* in the future; still far off

動　みたいで ☞ みたいだ / 誘って ☞ 誘う *sasou* / くれたり ☞ くれる

注　This passage is taken from F-ko's journal. / Though 会社 means "company," it often refers to a person's workplace, especially an office. / 興味 means "interest," and 興味がある "to be interested." / The suffix みたいだ means "seems." / The たり suffix in 誘ってくれたり corresponds to "other things"; that is, the man shows his interest in F-ko not only by inviting her to meals. / As in 3e, じゃ is a contraction of では *de wa*. 年下のＴじゃ、結婚は先だ means "In the case of T, who's younger than me, marriage is still a long ways off." / The clause-ending particle し means roughly "too; in addition." It is often used when several clauses all exemplify the same thing. Two more examples appear in 3n.

文　On average, Japanese marry later than people in any other country, and college graduates are especially likely to marry late. Few young men of T's age and situation are married. F-ko, though, would be considered quite eligible.

---

**3j**

この進行中の浮気を、さりげなく嘘つき日記に書くときの快感がたまらない。

---

語　進行中 *shinkō-chū* now in progress / 浮気 *uwaki* infidelity / さりげなく casually; nonchalantly / 書くとき *kaku toki* when (she) writes / 快感 *kaikan* pleasure / たまらない extremely good

注　The original meaning of たまらない is "unbearable," but it has taken on the extended meaning of "unbearably good." / 浮気 is the object of the verb 書く.

**3k**

「今日はＴがコンパで遅い。私は会社の彼と、雰
囲気のあるバーへ。

語　今日 *kyō* today; tonight / コンパ party / 遅い *osoi* late
(arriving home) / 雰囲気のある *fun'iki no aru* having a
nice ambience / バー bar; drinking spot

注　A コンパ is a college party where the attendees share the
expenses. The word comes from the English "company."
/ 会社の彼 *kaisha no kare* literally means "he of the company," that is, "the man at the office." / 雰囲気 means
the atmosphere or mood of a place. As here, it often
refers to an interesting, memorable, or romantic ambience. / With the omitted verb, the second sentence would
end バーへ行った *bā e itta* "went to a bar."

文　Japanese has several words for places where alcoholic bev-
erages are sold and consumed. A バー or パブ serves
mainly whiskey, brandy, cocktails, and other Western
drinks and may have a stylish interior. A スナック or ス
ナックバー serves light meals in addition to drinks. A
飲み屋 *nomiya* is a Japanese-style drinking and eating establishment, and an 居酒屋 *izakaya* is an inexpensive version of the same. A ビヤホール serves mainly beer, while
a クラブ or ナイトクラブ is generally more expensive
and caters to businessmen on expense accounts. A fashion-
conscious young woman is likely to prefer a バー as
being trendier or more romantic while disdaining a 飲み
屋 or 居酒屋 as the province of drab older men.

31

店を出る際、彼の腕が私の肩にさりげなく回っ
たときは、新たな恋の予感を感じて……」

語　店を出る際 *mise o deru sai* when we left the bar / 腕 *ude* arm / 肩 *kata* shoulder / 回った *mawatta* encircled; wrapped around / 恋 *koi* love; romance / 予感 *yokan* presentiment; anticipation / 感じて *kanjite* felt

動　回った ☞ 回る *mawaru* / 感じて ☞ 感じる *kanjiru*

注　The word 店 can refer to almost any kind of retail establishment, including bars, restaurants, shops, boutiques, etc. / If completed, this sentence would end 感じていた "I felt." / The subjects of 出る are F子さん and 会社の彼, the subject of 回った is 彼の腕, and the subject of 感じて(いた) is 私 *watashi* "I."

**3m**

これも Ｆ子さんの "創作" と信じて疑わないＴ君は、「リアリティーあるよね。ゾクゾクしちゃう」と無邪気なもの。

語 これも this also / 信じて *shinjite* believed / 疑わない *utagawanai* does not doubt / リアリティーある has reality; is realistic / ゾクゾクしちゃう shiver with excitement / 無邪気なもの *mujaki na mono* innocent person

動 信じて ☞ 信じる *shinjiru* / 疑わない ☞ 疑う *utagau* / ゾクゾクしちゃう ☞ ぞくぞくしてしまう ☞ ぞくぞくする，しまう

注 これ refers to the passage quoted from F-ko's journal. / "創作" is in quotation marks because F-ko's journal was not really the "imaginative work" that F-ko pretended it was. / The と after "創作" and the と after T's statement are both the quoting と (see 1j). / これもＦ子さんの "創作" と信じて疑わないＴ君 means "T, who believed without a doubt that this was also F-ko's 'imaginative work.'" / Referring to T as a 無邪気なもの suggests that he is innocent and childishly unsuspecting of F-ko's unfaithfulness. / This sentence's omitted verb is the copula だった.

**3n**

「日記のおかげで、彼の行動は全面ガラス張りだし、私の浮気は完全フィクションってことになってるし。

語　日記のおかげで *nikki no okage de* thanks to the diary / 彼の行動 *kare no kōdō* his actions / 全面 *zenmen* completely; in every aspect / ガラス張り *garasubari* visible; exposed / 完全 completely; entirely

動　なってる ☞ なっている ☞ なる，いる

注　This sentence and 3o are what F-ko is thinking or saying. They are not taken from her journal. / The original meaning of ガラス張り is "lined with glass (and thus visible from the outside)." In its extended meaning, the word refers to information that is open to the public. Here, it indicates that F-ko knows everything T does because he records it all in his diary. / フィクションってことになってる is a contraction of フィクションということになっている *fikushon to iu koto ni natte iru* "it is supposed to be fiction." / As described in 3i, the clause-ending し's mean roughly "too; in addition" and are used when giving a nonexhaustive listing of examples or reasons that lead to a certain conclusion (whether clearly stated or not). Here, these clauses explain why F-ko cannot stop keeping her journal (3o).

---

**3o**

しばらく、この交換日記やめられないわ」

---

語　しばらく for a while / 交換日記 *kōkan nikki* [lit.] exchange diaries / やめられない cannot quit

動　やめられない ☞ やめられる ☞ やめる

注　The meaning of 交換日記 is explained by this story: a diary in which two people alternate entries, or diaries that two people show to each other. The practice of exchanging 交換日記 is most common among girls of elementary or junior-high-school age.

---

**3p**

したたかに笑うF子さんである。

---

語　したたかに shrewdly / 笑う *warau* laugh

注　This したたかに is echoed in the title of the story (see 3a).

# 4

**極道の娘婿**
<ruby>娘婿<rt>むすめむこ</rt></ruby>

*THE SON-IN-LAW OF THE MOB*

# 極道の娘婿

大阪のデザイナー、T君（二四）は、先日、妻・M子さん（二四）の出身地、北陸X市を初めて訪れた。

T君は、この里帰りを怖えていた。というのは、M子さんの父親は北陸でちょいと名の知れた暴力団の組長。結婚披露宴は大阪だったが、パンチパーマが並び、

「幸せを噛みしめるどころじゃなかった」

からである。

さて、特急列車が駅に着くと、いきなりパンチパーマの一団が目に飛び込んできた。

「お帰りなさいませっ！」

T君が降りると、口々に叫ぶ。組本部では宴会の用意ができていて、壁には襲名披露のように、

「T君とお嬢様を祝う」というようなことを大書した紙が張ってある。

# THE SON-IN-LAW OF THE MOB

The other day, T (24), a designer in Osaka, paid his first visit to X City in Hokuriku, the birthplace of his wife, M-ko (24).

T was dreading this visit to his wife's home. The reason for which is that M-ko's father is the boss of a yakuza gang not entirely unknown in Hokuriku, and at their wedding reception, even though it was held in Osaka, there had been so many guys with gangster haircuts standing around that, as T says, "I was in no mood to enjoy any marital bliss."

When their train arrived at the station, a troop of gangster haircuts suddenly came into view.

"Welcome ho-o-o-ome!" they all yelled as T got off the train.

A banquet had been prepared for them at the gang headquarters. A poster on the wall read "In Honor of T and the Young Miss" in huge letters, as though announcing the name of the Boss's successor.

　Ｔ君は逃げ出したくなったが、

「何回か体験したら免疫になるから」

　平然とするＭ子さんに諭されて着席した。

　宴は盛り上がり、お開きというときに、Ｔ君にマイクが渡された。緊張でうまく言葉が出ない。が、なんとか最後までこぎつけ、

「みなさま、これからもよろしくお願いします」

　と、いおうとしたとき、

「みなさま、これからもよろしくご指導願います」

　と、いってしまった。

　一同、拍手喝采。Ｔ君がこの世界に入る、と勘違いしたのだ。

「親分の跡継ぎができた」

「若親分でうちも安泰だ」

　こんな声があちこちから漏れ、親分は感極まって涙し始めた。

　困ったのがＴ君。大阪へ帰っても連日のように、

「いつ帰るのか。この世界でも修業は必要だから……」

　と、義父から電話が入り、ノイローゼ寸前である。

T was inclined to make a run for it, but he was persuaded to take his seat by the unperturbed M-ko, who told him, "After you've been through this a few times you develop a certain resistance to it."

The party was lively. As the ending time approached, T was handed a microphone. He was so nervous that he stumbled over his words. Somehow he managed to get to the end, but when he tried to say, "In the future, I hope to get to know you all," he instead blurted out, "In the future, I hope to benefit from your advice."

One and all applauded and cheered. They had mistaken T to mean that he was going to enter the world of organized crime.

Here and there voices could be heard:

"The Boss has a successor."

"With the Young Boss, we have no more worries."

The Boss himself was moved to tears.

T didn't know what to do. Even though they've returned to Osaka, he receives a call from his father-in-law nearly every day, asking, "When are you coming home? Even in our business you need time for training, you know."

T is on the verge of a nervous breakdown.

## 4a

*Title:* 極道の娘婿

語　極道 *gokudō* the underworld; organized crime / 娘婿 *musumemuko* son-in-law

注　The term 極道 refers to the netherworld of gambling, prostitution, drugs, and other vices. Here it specifically means Japanese organized crime—the yakuza.

## 4b

大阪のデザイナー、T君（二四）は、先日、妻・M子さん（二四）の出身地、北陸X市を初めて訪れた。

語　大阪 *Ōsaka* Japan's second-largest city / デザイナー designer / T君 *Tī-kun* Mr. T (see 3b) / 先日 *senjitsu* the other day / 妻 *tsuma* wife / 出身地 *shusshin-chi* native area; birthplace / 北陸 *Hokuriku* the Japan Sea coastal area of central Japan / X市 *ekkusu-shi* X City / 初めて *hajimete* for the first time / 訪れた *otozureta* visited

動　訪れた ☞ 訪れる *otozureru*

注　The dot separating 妻 and M子さん is called a 中黒 *nakaguro* or 黒丸 *kuromaru*. Here it functions similarly to a comma, so 妻・M子さん means "his wife, M-ko." / 北陸 encompasses the prefectures of 新潟 *Niigata*, 富山 *Toyama*, 石川 *Ishikawa*, and 福井 *Fukui*. It is also called 北陸地方 *Hokuriku Chihō* "Hokuriku Region." / The comma after 出身地 is like an equals sign, indicating that X City in Hokuriku is M-ko's home town.

文 Jobs such as デザイナー fall into the general category of カタカナ職業 *katakana shokugyō*, that is, job titles written in katakana. Other examples include プロデューサー "producer," ディレクター "director," and ライター "writer." These titles convey the image of urban sophisticates who work in trendy, media-related fields, far from the sleazy world of organized crime into which T has married. / By identifying the Hokuriku city as X市, the "Dekigotology" editors are being especially cautious to avoid identifying the location, since no Japanese names begin with X in romaji. This extra caution may be due to the gangster connection.

---

**4c**

T君は、この里帰りを怯えていた。

---

語 里帰り *satogaeri* a visit by a newlywed woman and her husband to her family / 怯えていた *obiete ita* feared; dreaded

動 怯えて ☞ 怯える *obieru* / いた ☞ いる

## 4d

というのは、M子さんの父親は北陸でちょいと
名の知れた暴力団の組長。

語　というのは *to iu no wa* because / 父親 *chichioya* father /
ちょいと slightly; somewhat / 名の知れた *na no shireta*
famous; well-known / 暴力団 *bōryoku-dan* criminal gang /
組長 *kumichō* leader

動　知れた ☞ 知れる *shireru*

注　というのは indicates that what follows is an explanation
of what came before. Here, 4d and 4e explain why T was
dreading the visit to his wife's family home (4c). / 北陸
でちょいと名の知れた暴力団 means "a gang known
somewhat in Hokuriku." / Although the literal meaning
of ちょいと is "slightly; somewhat," here the word is
used with ironic understatement to suggest that the gang
is actually quite well-known in Hokuriku. / 組長 refers to
the head of any group that is called a 組. Many yakuza
gangs have names ending in 組, including the largest, 山
口組 *Yamaguchi-gumi*. But there are also legitimate organizations called 組, so in other contexts 組長 may not refer
to a gang boss. / The copula だ is omitted from the end
of this sentence.

文　Japan has hundreds of criminal gangs, including some of
nationwide and international scope. Their activities include drug dealing, gun running, gambling, prostitution,
extortion and protection rackets, confidence scams, and legitimate businesses as well. Many gangs have long histo-
ries and well-established organizations built upon fierce
group loyalty. Among the general population, the gangs
are regarded with a mixture of respect, amusement, and

fear. A police crackdown has weakened their influence in recent years.

---

**4e**

結婚披露宴は大阪だったが、パンチパーマが並び、「幸せを噛みしめるどころじゃなかった」からである。

---

語　結婚披露宴 *kekkon hirōen* wedding reception / パンチパーマ (men with a) short, curly hairstyle / 並び *narabi* were lined up / 幸せ *shiawase* happiness / 噛みしめる *kamishimeru* to savor; to enjoy / どころじゃなかった *dokoro ja nakatta* I was far from...; I certainly didn't feel like... / から because

動　だった ☞ だ / 並び ☞ 並ぶ *narabu* / じゃなかった ☞ ではなかった ☞ ではない *de wa nai* ☞ である

注　披露 *hirō* means announcement, so the meaning of 結婚披露宴 is "a party announcing a wedding." Traditional Japanese wedding ceremonies are attended only by family members, and one purpose of the 披露宴 is to inform the invited guests that the nuptials really did take place as scheduled. / 結婚披露宴は大阪だった means "the wedding reception was held in Osaka." / The word パンチパーマ is a Japanese neologism taken from the English "punch" and "perm." T was frightened when he saw many men with パンチパーマ at his wedding reception because this hairstyle is common among yakuza. / Strictly speaking, パンチパーマ refers to the hairstyle itself, but here and in 4f it means men who have that hairstyle. / The word どころ followed by a negative verb indicates that something that might be considered normal is in fact unlikely or impossible. 幸せを噛みしめるどころじゃなかった can be translated as "Enjoying my happiness (at getting married) was the furthest thing from my mind." / The から indicates that this sentence completes the explanation begun with というのは in 4d. In other words, T had dreaded the trip to his wife's home because her father was a gang leader and there had been many gangsters at their wedding reception.

---

**4f**

さて、特急列車が駅に着くと、いきなりパンチパーマの一団が目に飛び込んできた。

---

語 さて (shows a change in topic) / 特急列車 *tokkyū ressha* express train / 駅 *eki* train station / 着く *tsuku* arrive / いきなり suddenly / パンチパーマの一団 *panchipāma no ichidan* a group of men with "punch perms" / 目に飛び込んできた *me ni tobikonde kita* leaped into sight

動 飛び込んで ☞ 飛び込む *tobikomu* / きた ☞ 来る *kuru*

注 さて here indicates that the focus of the story has shifted from the reasons for T's fears back to the visit to X City. / 特急 is an abbreviation for 特別急行 *tokubetsu kyūkō* "special express." / Although 列車 *ressha* and 電車 *densha* can both be translated as "train," they are not identical. 列車 refers to a series of train cars linked together, while a 電車 may consist of only one car. A 電車 is powered by electricity, while a 列車 could have a steam or diesel engine. / The と after 着く is the sequential と (see 1j). / 飛び込む means "to jump into." The idiom 目に飛び込む literally means "to jump into one's eyes," that is, "to appear suddenly."

---

**4g**

「お帰りなさいませっ！」Ｔ君が降りると、口々に叫ぶ。

語　お帰りなさいませっ！ *o-kaerinasai masett* Welcome home! / 降りる *oriru* get off (the train) / 口々に *kuchiguchi ni* with many voices / 叫ぶ *sakebu* to shout

注　お帰りなさいませ is an especially polite version of お帰りなさい *o-kaerinasai*, the usual greeting given to a family member who has just come home. An informal everyday version is お帰り *o-kaeri*. / The small っ in お帰りなさいませっ indicates an abrupt halting of the voice at the end of the greeting. Here it suggests tough yakuza speech. (This small final っ indicates a glottal stop; it is not pronounced *t* or *tsu*.) / The と after 降りる is the sequential と.

## 4h

組本部では宴会の用意ができていて、壁には襲名披露のように、「Ｔ君とお嬢様を祝う」というようなことを大書した紙が張ってある。

**語** 組本部 *kumi honbu* gang headquarters / 宴会 *enkai* party; banquet / 用意ができていて *yōi ga dekite ite* preparations were finished / 壁には *kabe ni wa* on the wall / 襲名 *shūmei* the naming of a successor / 披露 *hirō* announcement / のように *no yō ni* like; as if / お嬢様 *o-jō-sama* daughter (respectful) / 祝う *iwau* congratulate / というようなこと *to iu yō na koto* something like... / 大書した *taisho shita* written large / 紙 *kami* paper / 張ってある *hatte aru* was stuck (to the wall)

**動** できて ☞ できる / いて ☞ いる / 大書した ☞ 大書する *taisho suru* / 張って ☞ 張る *haru*

**注** The term 本部 is used by many companies and other organizations to designate a headquarters or main office. / The verb 大書した modifies 紙. The phrase 「Ｔ君とお嬢様を祝う」というようなことを大書した紙 means "a piece of paper on which something like 'Congratulations to T and the Young Miss' was written large." / The と in というような is the quoting と.

**文** Many titled positions in Japan, from those of kabuki actors and artisans to those of shop owners and gang bosses, are handed down from generation to generation, with each person in line receiving the same ceremonial name. When a son is not available to inherit a male title, it may go instead to an adopted son or son-in-law. The banner congratulating T and M-ko, with T's name written so prominently, looked like a 襲名披露 "announcement of succession," suggesting that the gangsters believed that T was joining the gang as their boss's heir.

---

**4i**

Ｔ君は逃げ出したくなったが、「何回か体験したら免疫になるから」平然とするＭ子さんに諭されて着席した。

---

**語** 逃げ出したくなった *nigedashitaku natta* felt like running away / 何回か *nankai ka* a few times / 体験したら *taiken shitara* after you have experienced (this) / 免疫になる *men'eki ni naru* you'll become immune / 平然とする *heizen to suru* unconcerned; indifferent / Ｍ子さんに諭されて *Emu-ko-san ni satosarete* was instructed by M-ko / 着席した *chakuseki shita* sat down

**動** 逃げ出したく ☞ 逃げ出したい ☞ 逃げ出す *nigedasu* / なった ☞ なる / 体験したら ☞ 体験する *taiken suru* / 諭されて ☞ 諭される ☞ 諭す *satosu* / 着席した ☞ 着席する *chakuseki suru*

**注** 逃げ出す means "to run away," so 逃げ出したい is "want to run away" and 逃げ出したくなった is "began to feel like running away." / The words 体験 *taiken* and 経験 *keiken* both mean "experience" and are sometimes interchangable, though 体験 usually refers to a specific incident that has made an impression on a person, while 経験 often refers more generally to a person's past or background. / 免疫 is the medical term for "immunity." It also has the extended meaning, as seen here, of "being accustomed to something." / Ｔ君 is the subject of the passive verb 諭されて and Ｍ子さん is the agent, so the gist of the sentence is "T was instructed by M-ko." / 諭す

means "to provide moral instruction (to an inferior)." Here the word is meant to be comical, because it makes M-ko seem like her husband's teacher. / T君 is the subject of 着席した.

---

**4j**

宴は盛り上がり、お開きというときに、T君に
マイクが渡された。

---

語 宴 *utage* banquet / 盛り上がり *moriagari* became lively / お開き *o-hiraki* the end of the party / マイク microphone / 渡された *watasareta* was handed

動 盛り上がり ☞ 盛り上がる *moriagaru* / 渡された ☞ 渡される ☞ 渡す *watasu*

注 An elegant word for "banquet" or "party," 宴 sounds ironic when describing a gathering of thugs. / Words such as 終わる *owaru* "to end" and 切る *kiru* "to cut" are taboo at weddings and other celebrations, so euphemisms are supposed to be used instead. Here, お開き is the polite substitute for 終わり *owari* "the end."

---

**4k**

緊張でうまく言葉が出ない。

---

語 緊張で *kinchō de* because of nervousness / うまく well / 言葉 *kotoba* words / 出ない *denai* don't come out

動 出ない ☞ 出る *deru*

注 The topic of this sentence is T君. / うまく言葉が出な

---

い means "he wasn't able to get the words out very well."

---

**41**

が、なんとか最後<sup>さいご</sup>までこぎつけ、「みなさま、こ
れからもよろしくお願<sup>ねが</sup>いします」と、いおうと
したとき、「みなさま、これからもよろしくご指<sup>し</sup>
導願<sup>どうねが</sup>います」と、いってしまった。

---

語　が but; however / なんとか somehow or other / 最後ま
で *saigo made* until the end / こぎつけ he reached the
end / みなさま *mina-sama* you (plural, polite) / これか
らも *kore kara mo* from here on; in the future, too / よ
ろしくお願いします *yoroshiku o-negai shimasu* (see explanation below) / いおうとしたとき *iō to shita toki* when
he tried to say / ご指導願います *go-shidō negaimasu*
please give me instruction / いってしまった *itte shimatta*
he said (to his regret)

動　こぎつけ ☞ 漕ぎ着ける *kogitsukeru* / いおう, いって
☞ 言う *iu, yū* / した ☞ する / しまった ☞ しまう

注　The original meaning of 漕ぎ着ける is "to row (a boat)
all the way to one's destination." Here it is used in its extended meaning, "to reach a goal after repeated efforts." /
よろしくお願いします is a set phrase used when one is
introduced to other people. T had intended to close his
speech with this phrase. Instead, he said よろしくご指導
願います, which sounded as if he were asking the gangsters to instruct him in the ways of the underworld. /
The いおう in いおうとした is the informal volitional
form of 言う "to say." When the informal volitional is
followed by とする, it takes on the meaning "to try" in
the sense of "to attempt (without success)." / As explained

---

in 3h, the gerund + しまう pattern indicates that the action of the verb had unfortunate consequences. Here, T's slip of the tongue made the mobsters think that T intended to join them, a misinterpretation that was definitely unfortunate for T.

---

**4m**

一同、拍手喝采。Ｔ君がこの世界に入る、と勘違いしたのだ。

---

語　一同 *ichidō* everyone / 拍手喝采 *hakushu kassai* clapped and cheered / この世界 *kono sekai* this world (of organized crime) / 入る *hairu* enter; join / 勘違いした *kanchigai shita* misunderstood

動　勘違いした ☞ 勘違いする *kanchigai suru*

注　一同 means "everyone who was present" or "the entire group." / The omitted verb after 拍手喝采 is した. / 一同 is the subject of both 拍手喝采した and 勘違いした. / Ｔ君 is the subject of 入る. / The と before 勘違い is the quoting と (1j); it is used with the verb 勘違いした to indicate what was misunderstood. / The の in 勘違いしたのだ indicates that this sentence is an explanation of why everyone applauded.

---

**4n**

「親分の跡継ぎができた」「若親分でうちも安泰だ」

---

語　親分 *oyabun* the Boss / 跡継ぎ *atotsugi* successor / でき

た has been created / 若親分で *waka-oyabun de* with the Young Boss / うち we; our gang / 安泰 *antai* safe; secure

動　できた ☞ できる

文　The gang members want T to be second-in-line to M-ko's father because a son-in-law is more likely to be recognized as the undisputed leader of the gang should the current Boss be incapacitated. Without a designated heir, the gang would risk disintegration into rival factions. Many men join yakuza gangs because they come from broken families, have limited educations, or suffer other disadvantages that exclude them from mainstream Japanese life. Gangs bring structure and security to the members' lives.

---

## 4o

こんな声があちこちから漏れ、親分は感極まって涙し始めた。

---

語　こんな声 *konna koe* such voices; such words / あちこちから *achikochi kara* from here and there / 漏れ could be heard / 感極まって *kan-kiwamatte* was very moved / 涙し始めた *namida shi-hajimeta* began to shed tears

動　漏れ ☞ 漏れる *moreru* / 感極まって ☞ 感極まる *kan-kiwamaru* / 涙し ☞ 涙する *namida suru* / 始めた ☞ 始める *hajimeru*

注　こんな声 refers to the gangsters' outbursts of emotion in 4n. / The noun 涙 means "tears" and the verb 涙する "to shed tears."

---

**4p**

困ったのがＴ君。大阪へ帰っても連日のように、「いつ帰るのか。この世界でも修業は必要だから……」と、義父から電話が入り、ノイローゼ寸前である。

語　困ったの *komatta no* the one who didn't know what to do / 大阪へ帰っても *Ōsaka e kaette mo* even after they returned to Osaka / 連日のように *renjitsu no yō ni* nearly every day / いつ *itsu* when / 帰る *kaeru* come back (to X City) / この世界でも *kono sekai de mo* even in this business (of organized crime) / 修業 *shugyō* training; education / 必要 *hitsuyō* necessary / 義父 *gifu* father-in-law / 電話 *denwa* telephone call / ノイローゼ寸前 *noirōze sunzen* on the verge of a nervous breakdown

動　困った ☞ 困る *komaru* / 帰って ☞ 帰る *kaeru* / 入り ☞ 入る *hairu*

注　Here, 困る means "to be uncertain how to deal with an undesirable situation." / With the omitted verb shown, the first sentence would end Ｔ君だ. / 世界 is usually translated as "world." Here the sense is "field of activities," that is, the world of organized crime. / The から "because" after 必要だ shows that the clause explains something that was expressed or implied earlier. Here, the father-in-law wants T to come back to X City soon because a period of training is necessary even for people joining the underworld. / 電話が入り means "there were telephone calls (from the father-in-law nearly every day)." / The topic of ノイローゼ寸前である is Ｔ君. / ノイローゼ comes from the German *Neurose*, which is cognate with the English "neurosis." A Japanese synonym is 神経

症 *shinkei-shō* "nervous disorder." In informal speech and writing, ノイローゼ and 神経症 may refer to any of a wide and ill-defined range of emotional and mental problems. / 寸前 is a suffix meaning "just before; on the verge of." Other examples include 出発寸前 *shuppatsu sunzen* "just before departing" and ゴール寸前 *gōru sunzen* "just before (reaching) the goal."

文　At the end of this story, T faces the dilemma of balancing his own wish to keep away from the world of organized crime with his sense of family obligation to his new father-in-law. The difficulty of his dilemma is compounded by his spoken blunder, which made it seem as though he wanted to join the gang, and by the threat of violence that underlies most relations with yakuza.

# 5

## 潔癖OLの内柔外剛

### THE TWO SIDES OF A SUPERCLEAN WOMAN

# 潔癖ＯＬの内柔外剛

千代田区の大手出版社に勤めるＯ子さん（三四）は、きれい好きである。

外出には、傷口消毒薬を欠かさない。いまでは、洋式便座を拭（ぬぐ）う濡（ぬ）れナプキンが市販されているが、Ｏ子さんは十年以上も前から、傷口消毒薬を含ませたティッシュで拭（ふ）き拭きしていた。

トイレだけではない。新幹線に乗る時は、まず座席を拭き拭き。肘掛（ひじか）けはたびたび肌（はだ）が触れるので、特に念を入れる。他人の家に泊まるとなると、あてがわれた部屋の壁、窓のガラス、障子の桟（さん）、襖（ふすま）の引き手……。拭き拭きしないと眠れない。自宅でも、玄関のノブを毎度、拭いてから入るほどだ。

# THE TWO SIDES OF
## A SUPERCLEAN WOMAN

O-ko (24), who works for a large publishing company in Chiyoda-ku, likes things to be sparkling clean.

Whenever she goes out, she can't be without a disinfectant for minor cuts and scrapes. While moistened paper towels for wiping off Western-style toilet seats are now widely available, O-ko has been busily wiping toilet seats with tissue soaked in disinfectant for more than a decade.

And it's not just toilets. Whenever she takes the Shinkansen, the first thing she does is wipe off the seat. She's particularly careful with the armrests because of the repeated skin contact. When she stays at someone's home, she can't get to sleep until she has busily wiped everything in her room—the walls, the windows, the door frames, the door handles.... She even wipes the front door knob every time she goes into her own home.

　ところが、友人のA子さん（二八）が目撃した彼女の部屋は、洋服や本が散らばり放題。台所の床には、スリッパが張りついていた。卵を落として割ったときに、

「後で掃除すればいいや」

　と、何気なくスリッパをかぶせて何カ月も放っておいた。そのうち、接着剤でとめたように離れなくなったのだった。

「まあ、散らかってるけど、清潔よ。有機物やバクテリアは、消毒薬で拭き取ってる。卵から細菌が繁殖しても、空気中では休眠状態だから、こうすれば平気」

　といって、噴霧消毒剤のノズルをシューッと押したのだった。

　ちなみに、O子さんは東北大学薬学部の出身である。

But when her friend A-ko (28) got a look at O-ko's room, it was a complete mess—clothes and books scattered all around. There was a slipper plastered to the kitchen floor. When O-ko had dropped and broken an egg, she had simply put a slipper over it, thinking, "Oh, I can clean that up later." She left it there for several months, and before long the slipper had stuck fast, as if glued there.

"It may be messy, but it's clean," O-ko said. "I wipe up organic matter and bacteria with disinfectant. Even if germs should breed from the egg, they're still dormant in the air. There's no problem as long as I do this." As she spoke, she sprayed around some disinfectant.

Incidentally, O-ko graduated from the Faculty of Pharmaceutical Sciences at Tohoku University.

# COMMENTARY

## 5a

Title: <ruby>潔癖<rt>けっぺき</rt></ruby><ruby>ＯＬ<rt>オーエル</rt></ruby>の<ruby>内柔外剛<rt>ないじゅうがいごう</rt></ruby>

**語** 潔癖 *keppeki* obsessed with cleanliness; fastidious / OL *ōeru* female office worker / 内柔外剛 *naijūgaigō* tough on the outside but soft on the inside

**注** 潔癖 modifies OL. / OL is an abbreviation for the Japanese-English オフィス・レディー "office lady." The term indicates an office support worker who is female, usually young, and not in a career-track position. / The kanji in 内柔外剛 show the meaning: inside-soft-outside-tough, that is, lenient about matters that have to do with oneself but strict about matters that have to do with other people. A typical example would be a person who habitually eats junk food while urging others to watch their diets. Here, the 内 and 外 also refer literally to the protagonist's opposite attitudes toward germs inside and outside her home. This double meaning is indicated by the marks of emphasis that appear above 内 and 外 in the title on p. 94. These marks are called 傍点 *bōten* "side points," because they appear next to kanji in vertically printed text. The term 内柔外剛 appeared originally in 易経 *Ekikyō*, the Chinese classic of divination called the *Book of Changes* or *I Ching* in English. It is also written 外剛内柔 *gaigōnaijū*. The opposite is 外柔内剛 *gaijūnaigō* or 内剛外柔 *naigōgaijū*.

**5b**

千代田区の大手出版社に勤めるＯ子さん（三四）は、きれい好きである。

語　千代田区 *Chiyoda-ku* Chiyoda City (administrative area in central Tokyo) / 大手出版社 *ōte shuppansha* large publishing company / 勤める *tsutomeru* works; is employed / きれい好き *kirei-zuki* fond of cleanliness

注　Tokyo has twenty-three 区 *ku*. The word 区 has traditionally been translated as "ward," but in recent years many of Tokyo's 区 have changed their official English names to "city." / 大手 indicates a company that is one of the largest in its field.

**5c**

外出には、傷口消毒薬を欠かさない。

語　外出 *gaishutsu* going out; leaving home / 傷口 *kizuguchi* wound; injury / 消毒薬 *shōdoku-yaku* disinfectant / 欠かさない *kakasanai* does not omit; does not forget

動　欠かさない ☞ 欠かす *kakasu*

注　外出には *gaishutsu ni wa* here means "whenever O-ko goes out." The particle は is used for contrast to emphasize that O-ko's behavior is different when she's away from home. / 傷口消毒薬 is medical disinfectant for cleaning minor cuts and scrapes. / The verb 欠かす is often used, as here, in the negative. / The subject of this sentence is Ｏ子さん.

**5d**

いまでは、洋式便座を拭う濡れナプキンが市販されているが、O子さんは十年以上も前から、傷口消毒薬を含ませたティッシュで拭き拭きしていた。

語　いまでは *ima de wa* nowadays; these days / 洋式便座 *yōshiki benza* Western-style toilet seat / 拭う *nuguu* to wipe / 濡れナプキン *nure-napukin* moistened paper towels / 市販されている *shihan sarete iru* are sold (at retail stores); are marketed / 十年以上も前から *jūnen ijō mo mae kara* since more than ten years ago / 傷口消毒薬を含ませたティッシュ *kizuguchi shōdoku-yaku o fukumaseta tisshu* tissue soaked in disinfectant / 拭き拭きしていた *fukifuki shite ita* has wiped

動　市販されて ☞ 市販される ☞ 市販する *shihan suru* / 含ませた ☞ 含ませる ☞ 含む *fukumu* / 拭き拭きして ☞ 拭き拭きする *fukifuki suru* / いた ☞ いる

注　洋式便座を拭う濡れナプキン means "moistened paper towels for wiping off Western-style toilet seats." / 市販 refers only to selling in stores, markets, or other public venues. It is not used to describe private transactions. / The reduplicated 拭き拭きする suggests repeated, vigorous scrubbing and has a somewhat childish ring. The word is derived from the verb 拭く *fuku* "to wipe."

文　O-ko took special care to clean Western-style toilet seats because they come into direct contact with people's bottoms. With crouch-style Japanese toilets (和式トイレ *washiki toire*), the user does not touch the toilet. Although both types of toilet are common in Japan, the Western style is gaining popularity in both private homes and public facilities.

---

**5e**

トイレだけではない。新幹線に乗る時は、まず座席を拭き拭き。

語 　トイレ *toilets* / だけではない *dake de wa nai* not only / 新幹線 *Shinkansen* bullet train; Shinkansen / 乗る時は *noru toki wa* when she gets on (the Shinkansen) / まず first of all / 座席 *zaseki* the seat

注 　The subject of 乗る and 拭き拭き(する) is O子さん.

---

**5f**

肘掛けはたびたび肌が触れるので、特に念を入れる。

語 　肘掛け *hijikake* armrest / たびたび frequently; again and again / 肌 *hada* skin / 触れる *fureru* touches / ので because / 特に *toku ni* especially / 念を入れる *nen o ireru* is careful

注 　The 肘 *hiji* in 肘掛け means "elbow." / Other words ending in 掛け *kake* are 足掛け *ashikake* "footrest," 肩掛け *katakake* "shawl," and 洋服掛け *yōfukukake* "clothes hanger." / 念を入れる is a common idiom meaning "to be careful." 念 means "thought" or "feeling."

**5g**

他人の家に泊まるとなると、あてがわれた部屋
の壁、窓のガラス、障子の桟、襖の引き手……。

語 　他人 *tanin* another person / 家 *ie, uchi* house; home / 泊
まるとなると *tomaru to naru to* when she spends the
night / あてがわれた部屋 *ategawareta heya* the room as-
signed to her / 壁 *kabe* wall / 窓 *mado* window / ガラス
glass / 障子 *shōji* translucent sliding door / 桟 *san* lattice
/ 襖 *fusuma* opaque sliding door / 引き手 *hikite* handle

動 　あてがわれた ☞ あてがわれる ☞ あてがう

注 　Here, the kanji 家 might be read either いえ or うち. /
泊まる means "to spend the night; to stay." / The phrase
となると means roughly "when it is time to..." or "when
she happens to...." / あてがう means "to assign or allo-
cate to another person." / 障子 was originally the general
term for all traditional wood-frame sliding doors. Now
the word usually refers to 明かり障子 *akari shōji*, which
are covered with a single sheet of translucent paper, silk,
or plastic so that light can shine through. These 障子
have a framework of horizontal and vertical crossbeams
(桟) that one may hold when sliding the door open or
shut. A 襖 (or 襖障子 *fusuma shōji*) usually has no lattice
and is covered with two layers of paper, so light does not
pass through. The handle (引き手) is typically a round or
rectangular indentation.

---

**5h**

拭き拭きしないと眠れない。

---

語　拭き拭きしないと *fukifuki shinai to* if she doesn't busily wipe / 眠れない *nemurenai* she is unable to sleep

動　拭き拭きしない ☞ 拭き拭きする *fukifuki suru* / 眠れない ☞ 眠れる ☞ 眠る *nemuru*

---

**5i**

自宅でも、玄関のノブを毎度、拭いてから入るほどだ。

---

語　自宅でも *jitaku de mo* even at her own home / 玄関 *genkan* front door / ノブ knob / 毎度 *maido* every time / 拭いてから *fuite kara* after wiping / 入る *hairu* to enter / ほどだ *hodo da* she is so (fastidious that she...)

動　拭いて ☞ 拭く *fuku*

注　玄関 usually refers to the entranceway of a home or building, although here it refers specifically to the door itself. / The word ほど suggests that the action described by the sentence is somehow unusual or extreme. It can often be translated as "so (adjective) that...." In this case, the adjective is unstated, because we understand from the preceding sentences that what is being described is O-ko's obsession with cleanliness.

---

---

**5j**

ところが、友人のＡ子さん（二八）が目撃した
彼女の部屋は、洋服や本が散らばり放題。

---

語　ところが however (i.e., contrary to what one would ex-
pect) / 友人のＡ子さん *yūjin no Ē-ko-san* (O-ko's) friend,
A-ko / 目撃した *mokugeki shita* eyewitnessed; saw first-
hand / 彼女の部屋 *kanojo no heya* her room / 洋服
*yōfuku* clothing / 本 *hon* books / 散らばり放題 *chirabari
hōdai* scattered about with abandon

動　目撃した ☞ 目撃する *mokugeki suru* / 散らばり ☞ 散
らばる *chirabaru*

注　Ａ子さん is the subject of 目撃した, which modifies 部
屋. / 彼女 refers to Ｏ子さん. / 洋服 refers to dresses,
blouses, slacks, trousers, shirts, and other Western-style
clothing. The opposite is 和服 *wafuku* "Japanese-style
clothing." Since most Japanese wear 和服 only for special
occasions or not at all, 洋服 can usually be translated
merely as "clothing." / 散らばる means "to scatter
about." / The suffix 放題 is used after the *-masu* stems of
certain verbs to indicate that something is done with
complete freedom. Thus やり放題 *yari hōdai* means
"doing whatever you want" and 食べ放題 *tabe hōdai* "all
you can eat."

---

**5k**

台所の床には、スリッパが張りついていた。

---

語　台所 *daidokoro* kitchen / 床 *yuka* floor / スリッパ slipper / 張りついていた *haritsuite ita* was stuck

動　張りついて ☞ 張り付く *haritsuku* / いた ☞ いる

注　張り付く means "to be stuck firmly onto something."

文　In most Japanese homes, people wear slippers when walking on carpet, wood floors, or linoleum. They remove the slippers when walking on tatami, and switch to a different pair of slippers when using the toilet.

---

**51**

卵を落として割ったときに、「後で掃除すればいいや」と、何気なくスリッパをかぶせて何カ月も放っておいた。

---

語　卵 *tamago* egg / 落として割ったときに *otoshite watta toki ni* when she dropped and broke (an egg) / 後で掃除すればいいや *ato de sōji sureba ii ya* it's okay if I clean it later / 何げなく *nanige naku* casually; without concern / かぶせて covered up / 何カ月も *nankagetsu mo* for several months / 放っておいた *hōtte oita* had left untouched

動　落として ☞ 落とす *otosu* / 割った ☞ 割る *waru* / 掃除すれば ☞ 掃除する *sōji suru* / かぶせて ☞ 被せる *kabuseru* / 放って ☞ 放る *hōru* / おいた ☞ おく

注　The *-ba* form of a verb followed by いい "good" means "it's okay to do...," as in 後で掃除すればいいや. / The final や adds a sense of casual unconcern. This casualness is reinforced by the phrase 何げなく. / 放る here means "to leave alone; to ignore." / When used after a gerund, the verb おく adds the sense that the effects of the preceding verb extend into the future. Here おく is used because O-ko left the slipper stuck to the floor for months.

---

**5m**

そのうち、接着剤でとめたように離れなくなったのだった。

---

語　そのうち before long / 接着剤 *setchakuzai* adhesive; glue / とめたように as if attached / 離れなくなった *hanarenaku natta* became unable to detach

動　とめた ☞ とめる / 離れなく ☞ 離れない ☞ 離れる *hanareru* / なった ☞ なる / だった ☞ だ

注　接着剤でとめたように *setchakuzai de tometa yō ni* means "as if stuck with adhesive." / The の in 離れなくなったのだった shows that this sentence completes the explanation of why the slipper back in 5k was stuck to the floor.

---

**5n**

「まあ、散らかってるけど、清潔よ。

---

語　まあ well; anyway / 散らかってるけど *chirakatte 'ru kedo* it's messy, but / 清潔 *seiketsu* clean; hygienic

動　散らかってる ☞ 散らかっている ☞ 散らかる *chirakaru*

注　散らかる means "to be messy; to have things scattered about." People often use this word when apologizing to guests about a disorderly home. / 清潔 is close in meaning to 綺麗 *kirei* "clean; beautiful," but while 綺麗 may emphasize the clean appearance of something, 清潔 focuses on its healthful, hygienic cleanliness. As with the ね in 3e, the sentence-ending particle よ immediately after the adjectival noun 清潔 is an indicator of women's speech. A man would say 清潔だよ. A similar example of female usage is 平気 in 5p.

---

**5o**

有機物やバクテリアは、消毒薬で拭き取ってる。

---

語　有機物 *yūkibutsu* organic matter / バクテリア bacteria / 拭き取ってる *fukitotte 'ru* I wipe away

動　拭き取ってる ☞ 拭き取っている ☞ 拭き取る *fukitoru*

注　拭き取る means "to wipe off; to wipe away." / The subject of 拭き取ってる is the unspoken 私 *watashi*, meaning ○子さん. / Note that 有機物 and バクテリア are the objects of the verb 拭き取ってる.

## 5p

卵<ruby>卵<rt>たまご</rt></ruby>から細菌<ruby>細菌<rt>さいきん</rt></ruby>が繁殖<ruby>繁殖<rt>はんしょく</rt></ruby>しても、空気中<ruby>空気中<rt>くうきちゅう</rt></ruby>では休眠状<ruby>休眠状<rt>きゅうみんじょう</rt></ruby>態<ruby>態<rt>たい</rt></ruby>だから、こうすれば平気<ruby>平気<rt>へいき</rt></ruby>」といって、

語　細菌 *saikin* bacteria / 繁殖しても *hanshoku shite mo* even if (bacteria) propagate / 空気中では *kūkichū de wa* in the air / 休眠状態 *kyūmin jōtai* state of dormancy / こうすれば *kō sureba* if I do this / 平気 *heiki* okay; no problem / といって *to itte* she said

動　繁殖して ☞ 繁殖する *hanshoku suru* / すれば ☞ する / いって ☞ 言う *iu, yū*

注　平気 is used in speech to mean "there is no need to worry" or "I don't care." / Here, a man would more likely say 平気だ.

## 5q

噴霧消毒薬<ruby>噴霧消毒薬<rt>ふんむしょうどくやく</rt></ruby>のノズルをシューッと押<ruby>押<rt>お</rt></ruby>したのだった。

語　噴霧消毒薬 *funmu shōdoku-yaku* disinfectant vaporizor / ノズル nozzle / シューッと (indicates the sound of disinfectant being sprayed) / 押した *oshita* pushed

動　押した ☞ 押す *osu* / だった ☞ だ

注　噴霧 literally means "spraying fog." / The context suggests that 噴霧消毒薬 is the container for spraying the disinfectant, not the disinfectant itself. / The の in 押したのだった indicates that this sentence explains that こ

うすれば in 5p refers to O-ko's spraying the air with disinfectant.

---

**5r**

ちなみに、〇子さんは東北大学薬学部の出身である。

---

語 ちなみに incidentally; by the way / 東北大学 *Tōhoku Daigaku* Tohoku University / 薬学部 *Yakugaku-bu* Faculty Pharmaceutical Sciences / 出身 *shusshin* graduated from

注 東北大学 is a respected national university located in Sendai in northern Honshu. / In 4b, 出身地 *shusshin-chi* meant "the place where one was raised." Here, 出身 indicates the school from which O-ko graduated.

文 The point of this story is the contrast between O-ko's extreme aversion to possible sources of infection in public and her slovenly, unhygienic lifestyle at home. But behind this humorous situation is the more serious theme of the nearly pathological fear of germs that seems to affect an increasing number of Japanese. Sales of pens, computer keyboards, and other products made with antibacterial plastics have been booming, and surveys have reported that a significant percentage of people, especially women, never use public rest rooms. While some scientists warn that it is futile and even counterproductive to try to avoid contact with microorganisms, the spread of AIDS and some food poisoning scares have only increased people's fears. Despite these trends, though, O-ko's case is still unusual.

# 6

## ゼロ歳児にも及ぶ
## 受験戦争子守歌

*EXAMINATION HELL LULLABIES*
*FOR INFANTS*

# ゼロ歳児にも及ぶ
# 受験戦争子守歌

受験戦争といえば、いまや中学校や小学校の時代である。

　千葉に住むＳちゃん、生後十一カ月の両親は、昨今の情勢に遅れてはならぬ、とさっそく準備を開始した。

　母親の担当は"情操教育"。散歩の道すがら、

「ほら、あの女の子、隣の男の子に砂をかけてるでしょ。ダメよ、あんな子と付き合っちゃ」

「あっちのお母さんのお目め、不自然でしょ。きっと整形してる。ママみたいな自然の二重がいちばんなのよ」

　といった調子で、言い聞かせている。

　一方、お勉強担当の父親は、毎晩、枕元で最終目標の大学に向けて、「大学入学案内」や「大学の特色」を読み聞かせている。これをやると、Ｓちゃんは寝つきがいいそうだ。

# EXAMINATION HELL LULLABIES FOR INFANTS

These days, "examination hell" begins as early as junior high school or elementary school.

In Chiba, the parents of Baby S, eleven months old, have already commenced preparations, determined not to fall behind the times.

The mother is in charge of "moral and aesthetic education." While out for a walk, she lectures her son.

"Look!" she'll say. "That girl is throwing sand on the boy next to her. Never make friends with anyone like that."

"That mother's eyes look funny, don't they? I'm sure she had them fixed. It's better to have eyes with two natural folds like mine."

The father is in charge of the baby's studies. Looking ahead to the boy's ultimate admission to university, he reads college guidebooks at his son's bedside every evening. He says the boy falls asleep better that way.

　そんなある日、Ｓちゃんは一人で遊んでいて、入学案内をビリビリに破ってしまった。

　がっかりした父親だったが、ちりぢりになった本を見て驚いた。なんと、父親の出身校、慶応大学のページだけは破れていなかったのだ。

　で、息子の志望校は慶応と決め、まずは幼稚舎受験に全力を挙げることで夫婦の意見は一致。試験に輪投げがあったと聞いて、輪を握らせるのに必死になっている。

One day when Baby S was playing alone, he tore up one of the admission guidebooks.

The father was disappointed, but he was surprised when he saw the tattered book. Why, the only page left untouched was the one for Keio University, the father's alma mater!

So they decided that their son would aim for Keio. The parents agreed to focus all their efforts on the entrance exam for the university's nursery school. They've heard that the exam includes a ringtoss game, so they're doing everything they can to get their baby to wrap his fingers around a ring.

## 6a

*Title:* ゼロ歳児にも及ぶ受験戦争子守歌

語　ゼロ歳児 *zero-sai-ji* zero-year-old baby / にも及ぶ *ni mo oyobu* extending even to... / 受験戦争 *juken sensō* intense competition to pass entrance examinations; "examination hell" / 子守歌 *komori-uta* lullaby

注　In Japan, babies under the age of one are said to be ゼロ歳 *zero-sai* or 零歳 *rei-sai* "zero years old." / The word 受験 *juken* refers to studying for and taking examinations, especially college entrance tests. 戦争 *sensō* means "war." / A 子守歌 is a song sung to babies to put them to sleep. Here the word is used ironically. / This title literally means "Lullabies for Examination Hell, Which Now Reaches Even Infants Less Than a Year Old."

## 6b

受験戦争といえば、いまや中学校や小学校の時代である。

語　といえば *to ieba* concerning; in regard to; speaking of / いまや now / 中学校 *chūgakkō* junior high school / 小学校 *shōgakkō* elementary school / 時代 *jidai* era; age

動　いえば ☞ 言う *iu, yū*

注　といえば follows a subject that is already known or has been mentioned; it introduces information that is related (perhaps only tangentially) to that subject. Here, 受験戦争 is already known to the reader, and といえば indicates that the story that follows is somehow related to 受験戦争. / The point of this sentence is that high school students are no longer the only ones competing intensely to pass entrance examinations. Now junior high and elementary school students are also fighting the 受験戦争.

文　Japanese schools follow the six-three-three pattern introduced from the United States after the Second World War. 小学校 lasts for six years, followed by three years of 中学校 and three years of 高校 *kōkō* "high school."

---

**6c**

千葉に住むＳちゃん、生後十一カ月の両親は、昨今の情勢に遅れてはならぬ、とさっそく準備を開始した。

---

語　千葉 *Chiba* prefecture and city east of Tokyo / 住む *sumu* to live; to reside / ちゃん (respect suffix used with children's names) / 生後十一カ月 *seigo juikkagetsu* eleven months after birth / 両親 *ryōshin* parents / 昨今の情勢 *sakkon no jōsei* the current situation / 遅れてはならぬ *okurete wa naranu* must not delay / さっそく promptly / 準備 *junbi* preparations / 開始した *kaishi shita* commenced

動　遅れて ☞ 遅れる *okureru* / ならぬ (=ならない) ☞ なる / 開始した ☞ 開始する *kaishi suru*

注　千葉 might be either 千葉市 *Chiba-shi* "Chiba City" or

---

the larger 千葉県 *Chiba-ken* "Chiba Prefecture." / The ちゃん in Sちゃん is the version of さん used when addressing or talking about babies, children, and sometimes adults who are close friends or relatives, usually younger in age. Though ちゃん may be used for both males and females, it is more common with the latter. The equivalent suffix for males is 君 *kun* (see 3b). In this story, Sちゃん happens to be a boy (see 6o). / The quoting と after 昨今の情勢に遅れてはならぬ indicates that this sentence expresses the sentiments of S's parents, to wit, "we must not fall behind the times." / The final ぬ in ならぬ is the literary form of the negative suffix ない. The gerund (*-te* form) followed by either はならぬ *wa naranu* or はならない *wa naranai* means "must not." / Both 住む and 生後十一カ月 modify Sちゃん.

---

**6d**

母親の担当は"情操教育"。

語 母親 *hahaoya* mother / 担当 *tantō* (area of) responsibility / 情操教育 *jōsō kyōiku* moral and aesthetic education

注 情操教育 is a type of pedagogy that emphasizes the development of a child's overall sensitivity to moral, aesthetic, and spiritual matters. The quotation marks indicate that the term is being used sarcastically to refer to the less-than-lofty instruction provided by S's mother in 6e through 6i.

---

**6e**

散歩の道すがら、「ほら、あの女の子、隣の男の子に砂をかけてるでしょ。

語　散歩 *sanpo* walk; stroll / 道すがら *michi sugara* along the way / ほら hey! look! / あの女の子 *ano onna no ko* that girl / 隣の男の子に *tonari no otoko no ko ni* at the boy next to (her) / 砂 *suna* sand / かけてるでしょ *kakete 'ru desho* is throwing (sand), isn't she?

動　かけてる ☞ かけている ☞ かける

注　散歩の道すがら means "while taking a walk." / でしょ is an abbreviated spoken form of でしょう, the formal volitional form of the copula だ. / The subject of かけて(い)る is あの女の子.

---

**6f**

ダメよ、あんな子と付き合っちゃ」

語　ダメよ don't (do that) / あんな子と *anna ko to* with a child like that / 付き合っちゃ *tsukiatcha* (don't) be friends; (don't) spend time together

動　付き合っちゃ ☞ 付き合っては *tsukiatte wa* ☞ 付き合う *tsukiau*

注　The elements of this sentence have been reversed. In standard order and without the contraction to 付き合っちゃ, it would read あんな子と付き合ってはダメよ "Don't be friends with a girl like that." / A man would say ダメ

---

だよ instead of ダメよ. / Here ダメ is in katakana for emphasis. Also written だめ or 駄目, this word means "forbidden; no good; worthless."

---

### 6g

「あっちのお母さんのお目め、不自然でしょ。

語 あっちのお母さん *atchi no okāsan* that mother over there / お目め *o-meme* eyes / 不自然 *fushizen* unnatural

注 あっち is an informal version of あちら "that; over there." / お目め is a word used only by or to small children. Other children's words include お手て *o-tete* "hand," わんわん "dog," and ぶうぶう "automobile."

---

### 6h

きっと整形してる。ママみたいな自然の二重がいちばんなのよ」

語 きっと certainly; I'm sure / 整形してる *seikei shite 'ru* she's had plastic surgery / ママみたいな *Mama mitai na* like Mama's / 自然の *shizen no* natural / 二重 *futae* folded (eyelids) / いちばん the best

動 整形してる ☞ 整形している ☞ 整形する *seikei suru*

注 整形 can refer to any type of surgery or treatment that changes the shape of a part of a person's body. / Note that S's mother says ママ when talking about herself. When speaking to children, Japanese adults often refer to themselves by name or title rather than with a first-person

---

pronoun. Similarly, children usually refer to themselves by name until they reach school age, when girls are supposed to start saying 私 *watashi* and boys 僕 *boku* for "I; me." / 二重 here refers to 二重瞼 *futae mabuta* "double eyelids," that is, eyelids with a horizontal crease.

文 Most East Asians have 一重瞼 *hitoe mabuta* "single eyelids," that is, eyelids without a visible fold. Some Japanese who admire European facial features undergo a simple operation to add creases to their eyelids. Here, S's mother is sneering at another mother for having had that operation while bragging that her own eyelids are naturally the fashionable creased type. She may also be warning her infant son to avoid potential marriage partners who alter their appearance artificially.

---

**6i**

といった調子で、言い聞かせている。

語 といった調子で *to itta chōshi de* in this manner / 言い聞かせている *iikikasete iru* instructs

動 いった ☞ 言う *iu, yū* / 言い聞かせて ☞ 言い聞かせる *iikikaseru*

注 This sentence's initial と is the quoting と. It refers to the quotations from the mother in 6e through 6h. / 言い聞かせる means "to instruct" or "to convince." Here it seems to suggest that eleven-month-old S is actually paying attention to what his mother is saying.

**6j**

一方、お勉強担当の父親は、毎晩、枕元で最終目標の大学に向けて、「大学入学案内」や「入学の特色」を読み聞かせている。

語　一方 *ippō* meanwhile; on the other hand / お勉強担当の *o-benkyō tantō no* in charge of study / 父親 *chichioya* father / 毎晩 *maiban* every evening / 枕元で *makuramoto de* at (S's) bedside / 最終目標 *saishū mokuhyō* final goal; ultimate target / 大学 *daigaku* university / に向けて *ni mukete* directed toward; aiming at / 「大学入学案内」 *Daigaku Nyūgaku Annai* "Guide to University Admissions" / 「入学の特色」 *Nyūgaku no Tokushoku* "Key Features of Admissions" / 読み聞かせている *yomikikasete iru* reads to

動　読み聞かせて ☞ 読み聞かせる *yomikikaseru*

注　お勉強 has the prefix お because the word refers to a child's studies. / The 枕 *makura* in 枕元 means "pillow," and 枕元 literally means "next to the pillow." / 最終目標の大学 refers to the university that the parents want S to enter. / 大学入学案内 and 入学の特色 are commercially published guides to techniques for entering certain universities. 特色 means "unique characteristics." / 読み聞かせる means "to read to" or "to instruct through reading."

**6k**

これをやると、Sちゃんは寝つきがいいそうだ。

語 これをやると *kore o yaru to* when (the father) does this / 寝つきがいい *netsuki ga ii* falls asleep well / そうだ *sō da* is said to

注 これ refers to the father's reading to S. / The noun 寝つき "falling asleep" comes from the verb 寝つく *netsuku* "to fall asleep." / The word そう indicates reported speech. Here, it means that the parents have said that S falls sound asleep when they read the university admission books to him.

---

**61**

そんなある日、Ｓちゃんは一人で遊んでいて、入学案内をビリビリに破ってしまった。

---

語 そんなある日 *sonna aru hi* on one such day / 一人で遊んでいて *hitori de asonde ite* was playing alone / ビリビリに破ってしまった *biribiri ni yabutte shimatta* tore up

動 遊んでいて ☞ 遊ぶ *asobu* / 破って ☞ 破る *yaburu* / しまった ☞ しまう

注 Both そんな and ある modify 日. そんな日 means "such a day" and ある日 means "one day; on a certain day," so そんなある日 means "on one such day (during the baby's training for university admission)." / 入学案内 *Nyūgaku Annai* is the same as 大学入学案内 in 6j. / ビリビリに破る means "to tear up; to tear into shreds." ビリビリに suggests that the baby tore up the book especially violently.

## 6m

がっかりした父親だったが、ちりぢりになった本を見て驚いた。

語　がっかりした *gakkari shita* disappointed / ちりぢりになった本 *chirijiri ni natta hon* the book, which had been scattered around in pieces / 見て *mite* when he saw / 驚いた *odoroita* he was surprised

動　がっかりした ☞ がっかりする *gakkari suru* / だった ☞ だ / なった ☞ なる / 見て ☞ 見る *miru* / 驚いた ☞ 驚く *odoroku*

注　The unspoken subject of this sentence is 父親, which is the same as the predicate noun in the first half of the sentence. Thus the first half can be translated literally as "He was a disappointed father."

## 6n

なんと、父親の出身校、慶応大学のページだけは破れていなかったのだ。

語　なんと *nan to* (expresses pleased surprise) / 出身校 *shusshinkō* alma mater / 慶応大学のページだけ *Keiō Daigaku no pēji dake* only the page for Keio University / 破れていなかった *yaburete inakatta* was not torn up

動　破れて ☞ 破れる *yabureru* / いなかった ☞ いない ☞ いる

注　As in 5r, 出身 *shusshin* means "graduated from." 校 is an abbreviation for 学校 *gakkō* "school." Thus 出身校 means "the school from which one graduated." / The appositive comma after 出身校 indicates that the school in question is 慶応大学. / The の at the end of this sentence explains that the father was surprised in 6m because only the page for Keio University was not torn up.

文　Keio University is an old and respected private university in Tokyo. It was founded by 福沢諭吉 Fukuzawa Yukichi (1834–1901), the educator, philosopher, and diplomat whose face appears on the 10,000-yen note. The university's full name is 慶応義塾大学 *Keiō Gijuku Daigaku*. 慶応 is the era name for the years 1865 to 1868.

---

**60**

で、息子の志望校は慶応と決め、まずは幼稚舎受験に全力を挙げることで夫婦の意見は一致。

---

語　で then; therefore / 息子 *musuko* son / 志望校 *shibōkō* (see 注, below) / 慶応と決め *Keiō to kime* decided on Keio / まずは *mazu wa* first; to begin with / 幼稚舎 *Yōchisha* name of nursery school / 全力を挙げることで *zenryoku o ageru koto de* to make a total effort / 夫婦 *fūfu* the husband and wife / 意見 *iken* opinions / 一致 *itchi* matched; agreed

動　決め ☞ 決める *kimeru*

注　志望 *shibō* means "aspiration and desire," so 息子の志望校 means "the school their son would try to enter." / 幼稚舎受験 means "taking the nursery school entrance exams." 幼稚舎 is a nursery school affiliated with Keio

---

University and famous for its rigorous admittance standards. A child accepted by this nursery school is likely to be admitted to the university more easily. / The omitted verb at the end of this sentence is した. 夫婦の意見は一致した means "the opinions of the husband and wife were the same."

---

**6p**

試験に輪投げがあったと聞いて、輪を握らせるのに必死になっている。

---

語　試験 *shiken* test / 輪投げ *wanage* ringtoss / と聞いて *to kiite* they heard that / 輪 *wa* ring / 握らせるの *nigiraseru no* making him grasp / 必死になっている *hisshi ni natte iru* (they are) frantic

動　あった ☞ ある / 聞いて ☞ 聞く *kiku* / 握らせる ☞ 握る *nigiru* / なって ☞ なる

注　輪投げ is the children's game in which a ring made of rope, wood, or plastic is thrown from a distance onto a vertical pole. It is the type of game that might be included in a nursery school entrance examination. / 握らせる is the causative form of the verb 握る "to grasp; to hold." An eleven-month-old baby is too young to play ringtoss, so the parents are just trying to get him to wrap his fingers around the rings. / The の after 握らせる is the nominalizing の; it turns 握らせる into a noun.

文　While some people will be amused by the misplaced fervor of this mother and father eagerly trying to prepare their infant son for university entrance exams, for many Japanese parents this story may strike uncomfortably close to home. Among Japanese who fall into the broad social class of salaried white-collar workers—company employees, civil servants, academics, and the like—admission to a good university determines more than anything else one's career, social standing, and marriage prospects. Parents whose own lives have been shaped by this obsession with educational credentials are naturally eager for their own children to enter the best possible schools. The parents in this story are unusual not in the degree of their enthusiasm but only in how early they have begun.

つ

バン国目指す
コネ社員の無知蒙昧（もうまい）

THE CLUELESSNESS OF
A "CONNECTED" EMPLOYEE
ON HER WAY TO THE "COUNTRY OF BAN"

# バン国目指す
# コネ社員の無知蒙昧

都内の大手出版社に勤務するK嬢（二四）ほか同期の女性四人は、入社五年目を記念して、この春、一緒に海外旅行をする計画を立てた。

　候補地はいろいろ出たが、日数と予算から、シンガポールかタイのバンコク、ということで話はまとまった。

　翌日、K嬢は、会社の帰りに覗いた旅行代理店で、まさに理想的な日程と金額のタイのツアーを見つけ、とりあえず独断で予約を入れておいた。

　翌朝。仲間の一人のY嬢を見かけると、K嬢はさっそく、その件を報告した。

「いいのがあったのよ。勝手にタイのツアーを申し込んじゃったけれど、いいわよね」

# THE CLUELESSNESS OF
## A "CONNECTED" EMPLOYEE
### ON HER WAY TO THE "COUNTRY OF BAN"

This spring, Miss K (24) and three other women, her peers at a large publishing company in Tokyo, planned to take an overseas trip in honor of their fifth year since entering the company.

They discussed various destinations, but considering the available time and their budget, they settled on either Singapore or Bangkok, Thailand.

The next day, Miss K stopped at a travel agency on her way home from work and found a tour to Thailand with the ideal schedule and price. She went ahead and made the reservation.

The following morning, Miss K spotted one of the group, Miss Y, and immediately told her what she had done.

"I found a good tour, so I went ahead and signed us up for Thailand. That's okay, isn't it?"

　Ｙ嬢は意外な顔をし、軽い非難の調子を込めて答えた。

「あら、タイにしたの？バンコクじゃなかったの」

「えっ、だってバンコクはタイの首都だけど……」

「首都？えーっ、だってタイの首都はラオスでしょう。バンコクってコクがつくから国の名前じゃないの？」

「……」

　Ｙ嬢は生まれてこの方、二十四年間、バンコクはバンという国、つまり "バン国" と信じて疑わなかったのである。

（同期入社の女性社員に、一人だけ縁故採用者がいるという噂、本当だったんだ……）

　入社五年目にして、Ｋ嬢は噂の真偽を確信したのだった。

Miss Y looked surprised and replied in a somewhat critical tone, "What? Did you decide on Thailand? Weren't we going to Bangkok?"

"Huh? But Bangkok is the capital of Thailand...."

"The capital? But the capital of Thailand is Laos, isn't it? *Bankoku* ends in *koku*, so it must be the name of a country."

Miss K said nothing.

For the twenty-four years of her life, Miss Y had been convinced that the name Bangkok meant the "Country of Ban."

Miss K thought, *The rumor that one of the women hired with us got her job through a connection—I guess it was true after all.*

In her fifth year since joining the company, Miss K has now confirmed the truth of that rumor.

## 7a

*Title:* バン国目指すコネ社員の無知蒙昧

語　バン国 *Bankoku* the country of Ban / 目指す *mezasu* to aim for; to intend to go to / コネ connection / 社員 *shain* company employee / 無知蒙昧 *muchi-mōmai* ignorance

注　As the story explains, バン国 is a misinterpretation of バンコク "Bangkok." / The slanted line (ˋ) above the character 国 in the title on p. 130 indicates emphasis. See also 5a. / 目指す modifies 社員. / コネ is an abbreviation for コネクション, that is, a relative or friend who can provide special assistance or access. A コネ社員 is an employee who got her job through a personal introduction instead of the usual hiring process. (A typical コネ社員 might be the child of a former classmate of the company president.) / 無知 *muchi* means "no knowledge" and 蒙昧 *mōmai* "darkness; ignorance." 無知蒙昧 thus means "the depths of ignorance."

## 7b

都内の大手出版社に勤務するK嬢（二四）ほか同期の女性四人は、入社五年目を記念して、この春、一緒に海外旅行をする計画を立てた。

語　都内 *tonai* within Tokyo (see 3b) / 大手出版社 *ōte shup-*

*pansha* large publishing company (see 5b) / 勤務する works; is employed / K嬢 *Kei-jō* Miss K / ほか including (Miss K) / 同期の女性四人 *dōki no josei yonin* four women hired at the same time / 入社五年目 *nyūsha gonen-me* fifth year after entering the company / 記念して *kinen shite* in honor of / この春 *kono haru* this spring / 一緒に *issho ni* together / 海外旅行 *kaigai ryokō* overseas trip / 計画を立てた *keikaku o tateta* made a plan

動　記念して ☞ 記念する *kinen suru* / 立てた ☞ 立てる *tateru*

注　The suffix 嬢 in K嬢 is a title of respect for a young unmarried woman. Originally used for the daughters of the nobility and wealthy, now 嬢 is often applied with mild sarcasm in the popular press to young women who may put on high-class airs. / 同期 *dōki* means "same period of time," so K嬢ほか同期の女性四人 means "four women, including Miss K, who were hired at the same time."

文　Since large Japanese companies usually hire new employees only once a year, in April, the people hired at the same time tend to think of themselves as a group. And because there is no senior-junior (先輩 *senpai*, 後輩 *kōhai*) tension to color their relations, as there is with people hired earlier or later, 同期 employees often find it easier to socialize with each other than with other coworkers. / Because Miss K is twenty-four and just starting her fifth year of work, she and the other three women were probably hired immediately after they completed two years of junior college. This would traditionally make them 一般職 *ippanshoku*, the term used for support workers, especially women, who are not in line for promotion. In contrast, 総合職 *sōgōshoku* are career-track employees who, in large companies, are almost invariably graduates of four-year colleges. In recent years, more women have been attending four-year colleges and looking for 総合職 jobs, but they still do not always receive equal treatment in hiring and promotions.

---

**7c**

候補地はいろいろ出たが、日数と予算から、シンガポールかタイのバンコク、ということで話はまとまった。

---

語 候補地 *kōhochi* candidate locations / いろいろ various / 出た *deta* were mentioned; were proposed / 日数 *nissū* the number of days / 予算 *yosan* budget / から because of / シンガポールかタイのバンコク Singapore or Bangkok, Thailand / ということで *to iu koto de* (see 注, below) / 話はまとまった *hanashi wa matomatta* they decided; they reached a conclusion

動 出た ☞ 出る *deru* / まとまった ☞ まとまる

注 Thailand is called タイ in Japanese, while the Thai language is タイ語 *Tai-go*. / The phrase ということで refers to something that has been previously mentioned. It usually does not need to be translated into English.

---

**7d**

翌日、K嬢は、会社の帰りに覗いた旅行代理店で、まさに理想的な日程と金額のタイのツアーを見つけ、とりあえず独断で予約を入れておいた。

---

語　翌日 *yokujitsu* the next day / 会社の帰りに *kaisha no kaeri ni* on her way home from work / 覗いた *nozoita* peeked into; dropped by / 旅行代理店 *ryokō dairiten* travel agency / まさに *masa ni* exactly; precisely / 理想的な *risō-teki na* ideal / 日程 *nittei* schedule / 金額 *kingaku* amount of money / ツアー tour / 見つけ *mitsuke* she found / とりあえず provisionally; for the time being / 独断で *dokudan de* on her own judgment / 予約を入れておいた *yoyaku o irete oita* she went ahead and made a reservation

動　覗いた ☞ 覗く *nozoku* / 見つけ ☞ 見つける *mitsukeru* / 入れて ☞ 入れる *ireru* / おいた ☞ おく

注　覗いた modifies 旅行代理店, so 覗いた旅行代理店 means "a travel agency that she dropped by." / The use of とりあえず suggests that Miss K has made the reservation only provisionally, pending consultation with her coworkers. / The final おいた, translated above as "went ahead," indicates an action taken with an eye to future developments. See also 5l.

---

## 7e

翌朝。仲間の一人のＹ嬢を見かけると、Ｋ嬢はさっそく、その件を報告した。

語　翌朝 *yokuasa* the next morning / 仲間の一人のＹ嬢 *nakama no hitori no Wai-jō* Miss Y, one of the group / 見かける *mikakeru* notice; catch sight of / さっそく immediately / その件 *sono ken* that matter / 報告した *hōkoku shita* reported

動　報告した ☞ 報告する *hōkoku suru*

---

注　仲間 means "a companion, friend, or colleague (either individually or as a group)." / The と after 見かける is the sequential と (see 1j). / その件 here refers to the fact that Miss K had made a tour reservation. The word 件 is often used to refer to previously discussed matters.

---

**7f**

「いいのがあったのよ。勝手にタイのツアーを申し込んじゃったけれど、いいわよね」

---

語　いいのがあったのよ *ii no ga atta no yo* there was a good one / 勝手に *katte ni* on my own; without prior consultation or permission / 申し込んじゃった *mōshikonjatta* signed up for / いいわよね *ii wa yo ne* that's okay, isn't it?

動　あった ☞ ある / 申し込んじゃった ☞ 申し込んでしまった ☞ 申し込む *mōshikomu* / しまった ☞ しまう

注　When referring to a person's behavior, 勝手 usually suggests selfishness or disregard for the feelings of others. When it refers to the speaker's own actions, the word conveys a sense of humble apology. In this sentence, Miss K's apology for what she has done is reinforced by the しまった suffix (see 3h and 4l). This apology is little more than a ritual, though. Miss K in fact thinks she has done a good thing by making the reservation, and she is expecting to be thanked.

**7g**

Ｙ嬢は意外な顔をし、軽い非難の調子を込めて答えた。

語 意外な顔 *igai na kao* a surprised face / 軽い非難 *karui hinan* slight criticism / 調子 *chōshi* tone of voice / 込めて *komete* with; including / 答えた *kotaeta* answered

動 し ☞ する / 込めて ☞ 込める *komeru* / 答えた ☞ 答える *kotaeru*

注 意外な顔をする means "to make a surprised face" or "to look surprised." 意外 means "unexpected," and the reason for the surprise is that something unexpected has occurred.

## 7h

「あら、タイにしたの？バンコクじゃなかったの」

語 あら (shows mild surprise) / タイにしたの？ *Tai ni shita no?* Did you decide on Thailand? / バンコクじゃなかったの *Bankoku ja nakatta no* Wasn't it Bangkok?

動 した ☞ する / じゃなかった ☞ ではなかった ☞ ではない *de wa nai* ☞ である

注 The にする *ni suru* pattern means "to decide on; to choose." / In informal women's speech, a sentence ending with the particle の may be either an explanation or a question depending on the intonation. Explanatory の sentences have falling intonation, while questions have rising intonation. In writing, it is impossible to determine whether a sentence such as タイにしたの is an explanation or a question without contextual clues. Here, the ？ shows unambiguously that タイにしたの is a question, and that context tells the reader that バンコクじゃなかったの is a question as well. (Question marks are normally used in Japanese only in cases of possible ambiguity. If the sentence is clearly a question—because it ends in か, uses an interrogative pronoun, etc.—then the question mark is omitted.)

## 7i

「えっ、だってバンコクはタイの首都だけど……」

語 えっ *ett* Huh?! / だって but / 首都 *shuto* capital city

注　えっ is a shortened version of ええ, an interjection that, depending on the situation and intonation, can indicate joy, sorrow, anger, agreement, or hesitation. Here it shows surprise. As in 4g, the final small っ in えっ indicates a sudden halting of the vocal chords. It is not pronounced "t." Here and in 7j (えーっ), this っ is similar to an exclamation point. / The conjunction だって is used in speech when asserting a fact that contradicts another person's statement or assumption.

---

**7j**

「首都？えーっ、だってタイの首都はラオスでしょう。バンコクってコクがつくから国の名前じゃないの？」「……」

---

語　えーっ *ētt* (shows surprise or disbelief) / ラオス Laos / コクがつく *koku ga tsuku* ends in *koku* ("country") / 国の名前 *kuni no namae* the name of a country / じゃないの *ja nai no* isn't it?

動　じゃない ☞ ではない *de wa nai* ☞ である

注　えーっ is pronounced with a prolonged rising tone. This interjection is often used in conversation by young women. / The って after バンコク is a contraction of というのは *to iu no wa*, which literally means "that which is called...," though there is usually no need to translate it into English. In writing, バンコクというのは might be rendered with quotation marks: "Bangkok." / The ellipsis dots in quotation marks 「……」 indicate that the listener, Miss K, is so stunned she is unable to speak.

---

文 Genuine country names that end in 国 *koku* include 英国 *Eikoku* "United Kingdom," チリ共和国 *Chiri Kyō-wakoku* "Republic of Chile," and the official name of Japan, 日本国 *Nihonkoku* or *Nipponkoku*.

---

**7k**

Ｙ嬢は生まれてこの方、二十四年間、バンコクはバンという国、つまり "バン国" と信じて疑わなかったのである。

---

語 生まれてこの方 *umarete kono kata* ever since she was born / 二十四年間 *nijūyo nenkan* twenty-four years / バンという国 *Ban to iu kuni* a country called Ban / つまり in other words; that is / 信じて疑わなかった *shinjite utagawanakatta* believed and didn't doubt

動 生まれて ☞ 生まれる *umareru* / 信じて ☞ 信じる *shinjiru* / 疑わなかった ☞ 疑わない ☞ 疑う *utagau*

注 この方 *kono kata* means "since; after." 生まれてこの方 is a set phrase that means "all one's life; ever since one was born." / The と before 信じて is the quoting と, indicating what Miss Y believed. / Another version of the phrase 信じて疑わなかった appears in 3m.

**71**

（同期入社の女性社員に、一人だけ縁故採用者
がいるという噂、本当だったんだ……）

語　同期入社の女性社員に *dōki nyūsha no josei shain ni*
among the female employees who joined the company at
the same time / 一人だけ *hitori dake* only one (person) /
縁故採用者 *enko saiyōsha* a person hired through a personal connection / 噂 *uwasa* rumor / 本当だったんだ
*hontō datta n' da* was true

動　だった ☞ だ

注　縁故 means nearly the same thing as コネ in 7a—a personal connection, whether through blood, marriage, or acquaintance. / 採用する *saiyō suru* means "to hire," and
採用者 *saiyōsha* is "hiree." / 一人だけ縁故採用者がいる
という噂 *hitori dake enko saiyōsha ga iru to iu uwasa* means
"the rumor that only one person was hired through a
personal connection." / The ん in 本当だったんだ is a
contraction of the explanatory の. In other words, the
fact that there was one hiree—Miss Y—who got her job
through a connection explains why Miss Y is working in
this company even though she is so ignorant. / This sentence is in parentheses because it indicates Miss K's
thoughts.

**7m**

入社五年目にして、K嬢は噂の真偽を確信した
のだった。

語　入社五年目にして *nyūsha gonen-me ni shite* in the fifth
year after joining the company / 噂の真偽 *uwasa no
shingi* the truth of the rumor / 確信した *kakushin shita*
was convinced of

動　確信した ☞ 確信する *kakushin suru* / だった ☞ だ

注　にして is a literary version of に or で "in or at (a place
or time)." / The characters 真 and 偽 in 真偽 mean
"truth" and "falsehood," respectively. In some contexts, 真
偽 can be translated as "truth or falsehood," though here
just "truth" is better.

文　Large Japanese companies, which often have their pick of
new hires, screen prospective employees in several ways.
One is by choosing only those who have graduated from
high-ranked universities, thus relying on the rigor of the
university entrance exams to weed out the poorly edu-
cated and the less diligent. Another is by subjecting ap-
plicants to exams and interviews. The tests given by
companies are usually not as tough as college entrance
exams, and they often focus on more practical, common-
sense knowledge, such as current events and geography.
And a third is to use recommendations from the personal
contacts of important people in the company. While this
method is sometimes as effective as the others—a recom-
mender can lose face if the introduced employee turns
out to be a dud—it does not always work, as shown here
by the case of Miss Y.

# 8

## お坊っちゃま
## 飲尿健康法と恋人の憂鬱

### THE RICH BOY'S URINE THERAPY
### AND HIS GIRLFRIEND'S DEPRESSION

# ❽ お坊っちゃま
## 飲尿健康法と恋人の憂鬱

神奈川の住宅設計会社のOL、M子さん（二四）に、O君（二八）という吉川晃司似の恋人ができた。大学こそ二流だが、身長一八四センチ、父の経営する不動産会社に勤め、年収は八百万円を超す。車もBMWとパジェロを使い分けている。

M子さんは二月十四日、三万円のホンチョコを用意し、女友だちのカップルと横浜でダブルデートをした。その夜、二組のカップルは海の見えるホテルにチェックイン。

O君がシャワーを浴びているとき、隣の部屋の女友だちから電話があった。

「ねえ、私の彼が聞き出したんだけど、O君毎朝健康のためにおしっこ飲んでるんだって」

「げっ、マジ？」

# THE RICH BOY'S URINE THERAPY AND HIS GIRLFRIEND'S DEPRESSION

M-ko (24), an office worker at an architectural firm in Kanagawa, now has a boyfriend, O (28), who is as handsome as Kōji Kikkawa. Although he went to a second-rate university, he's 184 centimeters tall, works at a real estate company run by his father, and makes over eight million yen a year. He drives both a BMW and a Mitsubishi Pajero.

On Valentine's Day, M-ko bought 30,000 yen worth of chocolate just for O, and they went on a double date to Yokohama with another couple. That night, the two couples checked into a hotel with a view of the sea.

While O was taking a shower, M-ko got a telephone call from her girlfriend in the next room.

"Hey, according to my boyfriend, O drinks his own piss every morning. He says it's good for his health."

"Yuck!" M-ko said. "Are you serious?"

　M子さんが恐る恐るO君に聞くと、自信たっぷりに答えた。

「風邪も扁桃炎も花粉症もこれで治ったんだ。尿の成分は汗や涙と同じで、ちっとも汚くないんだ。君も飲んでみろよ」

　O君にキスされそうになったM子さんは、「キスは絶対にイヤ！」と頑なに拒んだ。

　O君は"ノーパン健康法"も取り入れていて、寝るときにはいつも下着をつけない。

　M子さんは三日間悩んだ末、O君に三つの条件を出した。

　①　私の前で飲尿しないこと
　②　私に飲尿を勧めないこと
　③　飲尿後は必ずうがいし、二十分以上歯を磨く
　　　こと

　かっこよく、優しく、お金持ちのO君は毎週末、高級レストランに誘ってくれる。しかし、M子さんは憂鬱だ。

「いま、飲んだワインが体内で温まり、彼は明日の朝また飲むんだわ」

　と想像するたびに、ご馳走がまずくなるからである。

When M-ko nervously asked O about it, he replied confidently, "It has cured my colds and tonsillitis and hay fever. There's nothing dirty about urine; it has the same components as sweat and tears. You should try drinking it, too."

When O started to kiss M-ko, she adamantly refused. "No kissing! No way!"

O also practices "no-underpants therapy"—he never wears briefs when he sleeps.

After stewing over it for three days, M-ko laid down three rules for O:

(1) Do not drink urine in front of me.

(2) Do not try to get me to drink urine.

(3) Always gargle after drinking urine, and then brush your teeth for at least twenty minutes.

Every weekend, the handsome, gentle, and rich O invites M-ko out to expensive restaurants. But M-ko just feels depressed.

"That wine he's drinking now will get warmed up in his body, and then tomorrow morning he's going to drink it again."

Whenever she thinks about it, the gourmet food turns bitter in her mouth.

# COMMENTARY

## 8a

*Title:* お坊っちゃま飲尿健康法と恋人の憂鬱

語 お坊ちゃま *o-botchama* rich boy / 飲尿健康法 *innyō kenkō-hō* urine therapy / 恋人 *koibito* girlfriend / 憂鬱 *yūutsu* depression; melancholy

注 お坊っちゃま is the extra polite version of お坊っちゃ ん *o-botchan*, which is either a polite term for another person's son or a derisive term for a rich, coddled young man who lacks common sense. / Just as ちゃん is a child's-language version of the polite suffix さん (6c), ち ゃま is the child's version of the even politer suffix さま. / As explained in this story, adherents of 飲尿健康法 believe that drinking or gargling one's own urine in the morning is beneficial to one's health in various ways. A few Japanese doctors advocate the practice, though it is not widely followed in Japan. / The characters in the phrase 飲尿健康法 mean "drink-urine-health-method." / A 恋人 may be either a boyfriend or a girlfriend. Unlike 愛人 *aijin* "lover," the word 恋人 does not imply— though it does not rule out—sexual intimacy. / If you like to impress people with your ability to write difficult kanji, the 鬱 in 憂鬱 is a good one to learn. (It is also written 欝. Learn both versions and impress people even more.)

## 8b

神奈川の住宅設計会社のＯＬ、Ｍ子さん（二四）
に、Ｏ君（二八）という吉川晃司似の恋人がで
きた。

**語** 神奈川 *Kanagawa* prefecture south of Tokyo / 住宅設計
会社 *jūtaku sekkei gaisha* housing design company / Ｏ Ｌ
*ōeru* female office worker (see 5a) / 吉川晃司似 *Kikkawa
Kōji-ni* resembling Kōji Kikkawa / 恋人ができた *koibito
ga dekita* (she) acquired a boyfriend

**動** できた ☞ できる

**注** 吉川晃司 is a handsome pop singer and actor. He was at
the height of his popularity in the early 1990s, when this
story was written. / The suffix 似 *ni* means "resembling;
looking like." / The いう in Ｏ君という modifes 恋人,
so Ｏ君という吉川晃司似の恋人 means "a boyfriend
named O who looks like Kōji Kikkawa." / The suffix 君
*kun* is explained in 3b.

**文** Articles in the popular press often describe people's appearance through comparisons with show business person-
alities.

**8c**

大学こそ二流だが、身長一八四センチ、父
の経営する不動産会社に勤め、年収は八百万円
を超す。

語 大学 *daigaku* university / こそ (adds emphasis) / 二流
*niryū* second-rate / 身長 *shinchō* height / 一八四センチ
*hyaku hachijū yon senchi* 184 centimeters (6'0") / 父 *chichi*
his father / 経営する *keiei suru* runs; manages / 不動産
会社 *fudōsan gaisha* real-estate company / 勤め *tsutome*
works; is employed / 年収 *nenshū* annual income / 八百
万円 *happyaku man en* eight million yen / 超す *kosu* ex-
ceeds

動 勤め ☞ 勤める *tsutomeru*

注 This sentence describes three things: O's education, his
height, and his income and job. While M-ko regards the
second and third—184 centimeters and eight million yen
per year from his father's company—as good, the first—O's
graduation from a second-rate university—is not so favor-
able. The particle こそ singles out 大学 as different from
the other two elements. / The particle の after 父 is an alternative form of the subject particle が, so 父の経営す
る不動産会社 means "the real-estate company that his father manages," with 父の経営する being a relative clause
that modifies 不動産会社.

文 This sentence assumed that the reader was in tune with
the Japanese zeitgeist of the early 1990s. At that time,
Japanese women were said to demand three things from
prospective husbands: 高学歴 *kō-gakureki* "high educational background," 高身長 *kō-shinchō* "high height," and

高収入 *kō-shūnyū* "high income." In other words, they were supposedly interested only in men who were tall and rich and had gone to good universities. Because each requirement began with the kanji 高, they were referred to collectively as 三高 *sankō* "the three highs." Like 吉川晃司, though, 三高 vanished from the public consciousness within a few years.

---

**8d**

車<sup>くるま</sup>もＢＭＷとパジェロを使<sup>つか</sup>い分<sup>わ</sup>けている。

---

語　車 *kuruma* cars / パジェロ *Pajero* / 使い分けている *tsukaiwakete iru* uses one or the other as appropriate

動　使い分けて ☞ 使い分ける *tsukaiwakeru*

注　The も "also" after 車 indicates that O's cars are another example of his wealth and attractiveness to M-ko. / Pajero is the name of a line of four-wheel-drive vehicles made by Mitsubishi Motors. In some countries they are marketed under the name Montero or Shogun.

## 8e

M子さんは二月十四日、三万円のホンチョコを用意し、女友だちのカップルと横浜でダブルデートをした。

語 二月十四日 *nigatsu jūyokka* February 14th (Valentine's Day) / 三万円 *san man en* (costing) thirty thousand yen / ホンチョコ a sincere present of chocolate / 用意し *yōi shi* prepared / 女友だち *onna tomodachi* girlfriend / カップル couple / 横浜 *Yokohama* city south of Tokyo, in Kanagawa Prefecture / ダブルデート double date

動 用意し ☞ 用意する *yōi suru* / した ☞ する

注 女友だち is a friend who happens to be a girl or woman. No romantic connection is implied. / In Japanese, the meaning of カップル is restricted to a man and woman who are lovers or married to each other. The word is not normally used in the more general sense of "pair."

文 On Valentine's Day, Japanese women give presents of chocolate to men. There are two major categories of these chocolate presents: 義理チョコ *giri choko* "obligatory chocolate," which includes inexpensive chocolate candies that female office workers give to male coworkers or bosses in whom they have no romantic interest, and ホンチョコ "favorite's chocolate," which is a more expensive chocolate gift given to an actual or prospective lover. The ホン in ホンチョコ is an abbreviation of 本命 *honmei*. Originally a sports term for a competitor that is expected to come in first in a race, 本命 can also refer to the person who is the leading candidate for some position. In this story, O is M-ko's leading candidate for her future husband. / March 14th has been designated ホワイトデー "White Day" in Japan. On that day, men who received Valentine presents are supposed to reciprocate with gifts of white chocolate or other treats.

---

**8f**

その夜、二組のカップルは海の見えるホテルにチェックイン。

---

語　その夜 *sono yoru* that night / 二組のカップル *futakumi no kappuru* the two couples / 海の見えるホテル *umi no mieru hoteru* a hotel with a view of the sea / チェックイン checked in

注　The の in 海の見える is an alternative to the potential particle が, so 海の見えるホテル literally means "a hotel from which the sea can be seen." / With the omitted verb added, this sentence would end チェックインした.

---

**8g**

O君がシャワーを浴びているとき、隣の部屋の女友だちから電話があった。

---

語　シャワーを浴びているとき *shawā o abite iru toki* while taking a shower / 隣の部屋 *tonari no heya* the room next door / 電話があった *denwa ga atta* there was a telephone call

動　浴びて ☞ 浴びる *abiru* / あった ☞ ある

注　シャワーを浴びる is the usual expression for "to take a shower." 浴びる means "to be drenched with a large amount of water or other liquid."

---

## 8h

「ねえ、私の彼が聞き出したんだけど、Ｏ君毎朝健康のためにおしっこ飲んでるんだって」

---

語　ねえ hey, listen! / 私の彼 *watashi no kare* my boyfriend / 聞き出した *kikidashita* extracted information by asking; found out / 毎朝 *maiasa* every morning / 健康のために *kenkō no tame ni* for health's sake / おしっこ urine / 飲んでるんだって *nonde 'ru n' datte* (is said to) drink

動　聞き出した ☞ 聞き出す *kikidasu* / 飲んでる ☞ 飲んでいる ☞ 飲む *nomu*

注　ねえ is used in conversation to get another person's attention or to change the subject to something that the speaker considers important. / Here 彼 means "boyfriend." Similarly, 彼女 *kanojo* sometimes means "girlfriend." / おしっこ is the word that children learn for "urine." A more formal word is 小便 *shōben*. The medical term is 尿 *nyō*. / The ん after 聞き出した and 飲んでる is a contraction of the explanatory and nominalizing の. / The ending って is used to report what someone else has said. It is a contraction of という.

---

**8i**

「げっ、マジ？」

---

語　げっ *gett* yuck! gross! / マジ really? are you serious?

注　The interjection げっ indicates the speaker's disgust. (The small っ is explained in 4g.) An initial げ seems to connote stomach upset in Japanese. Similar words include げろ "vomit," げっぷ "burp," and the onomatopoetic げえげえ, which describes the sound of retching. / マジ is a shortened, slangy version of 真面目 *majime* "serious; not joking."

---

**8j**

M子さんが恐る恐る O君に聞くと、自信たっぷりに答えた。

---

語　恐る恐る *osoru-osoru* nervously; fearfully / O君に聞くと *Ō-kun ni kiku to* when (M-ko) asked O / 自信たっぷりに *jishin tappuri ni* full of self-confidence / 答えた *kotaeta* answered

動　答えた ☞ 答える *kotaeru*

注　The reduplicated 恐る恐る is an adverb derived from the verb 恐る *osoru* "to fear." / The と after 聞く is the sequential と. / たっぷり means "full." / The subject of 答えた is O君.

---

---

**8k**

「風邪も扁桃炎も花粉症もこれで治ったんだ。

語 風邪 *kaze* a cold; the flu / 扁桃炎 *hentōen* tonsillitis / 花粉症 *kafunshō* pollen allergy; hay fever / これで by means of this / 治った *naotta* were cured

動 治った ☞ 治る *naoru*

注 風邪 can refer to both the common cold and the flu. / The tonsils are called 扁桃腺 *hentōsen*. / The verb なおる is written 治る when it means "to recover from an illness." When it means "to be repaired; to be restored," it is written 直る.

---

**8l**

尿の成分は汗や涙と同じで、ちっとも汚くないんだ。君も飲んでみろよ」

語 尿の成分 *nyō no seibun* the components of urine / 汗 *ase* sweat / 涙 *namida* tears / 同じ *onaji* the same / ちっとも (not) at all / 汚くない *kitanakunai* not dirty / 君 *kimi* you / 飲んでみろよ *nonde miro yo* try drinking it

動 で ☞ だ / 汚くない ☞ 汚い *kitanai* / 飲んで ☞ 飲む *nomu* / みろ ☞ みる

注 尿の成分は汗や涙と同じで means "urine is made of the same things as sweat and tears." / ちっとも adds emphasis to the meaning of a sentence. It is used only in negative constructions. / The pronoun 君 *kimi* is used

---

mainly by men when addressing a friend or close acquaintance who is of equal or lower social status. Being a woman, M-ko would be likely to reply to her boyfriend using either his name (probably followed by さん, ちゃん, or 君 *kun*) or あなた "you." / みろ is the brusque imperative form of みる. / When used after the gerund (*-te*) form, みる means "to try," so 飲んでみる is "to try drinking." / The final よ reinforces O's recommendation that M-ko try urine therapy.

---

**8m**

O君にキスされそうになったM子さんは、「キスは絶対にイヤ！」と頑なに拒んだ。

---

語　キスされそうになった *kisu saresō ni natta* was about to be kissed (by O) / 絶対に *zettai ni* absolutely / イヤ！ no! I refuse! / 頑なに *katakuna ni* stubbornly / 拒んだ *kobanda* refused

動　キスされ ☞ キスされる ☞ キスする / なった ☞ なる / 拒んだ ☞ 拒む *kobamu*

注　イヤ indicates strong dislike or refusal. It is also written いや, 嫌, or 厭. / The な in the adjectival noun (*na* adjective) 頑な *katakuna* is part of the stem, so another な is needed when the word precedes a noun: 頑なな態度 *katakuna na taido* "stubborn behavior."

## 8n

O君は "ノーパン健康法" も取り入れていて、寝るときにはいつも下着をつけない。

語　ノーパン健康法 *nōpan kenkōhō* no-underpants therapy / 取り入れていて *toriirete ite* has adopted / 寝るときには *neru toki ni wa* when he goes to bed / いつも always / 下着をつけない *shitagi o tsukenai* doesn't wear underwear

動　取り入れて ☞ 取り入れる *toriireru* / いて ☞ いる / つけない ☞ つける

注　The パン in ノーパン is an abbreviation of パンツ "underpants" or パンティー "panties."

文　Practitioners of ノーパン健康法 believe that sleeping without any restrictions on the nether regions is beneficial to one's health.

## 8o

M子さんは三日間悩んだ末、O君に三つの条件を出した。

語　三日間 *mikka kan* for three days / 悩んだ *nayanda* worried; was unable to decide / 末 *sue* after / 三つの条件 *mittsu no jōken* three conditions / 出した *dashita* presented

動　悩んだ ☞ 悩む *nayamu* / 出した ☞ 出す *dasu*

注　末 refers to the end of an action or period of time, so 三日間悩んだ末 means "after brooding over it for three days."

**8p**

① 私の前で飲尿しないこと

② 私に飲尿を勧めないこと

③ 飲尿後は必ずうがいし、二十分以上歯を磨くこと

語　私の前で *watashi no mae de* in front of me; in my presence / 飲尿しない *innyō shinai* do not drink urine / 勧めない *susumenai* do not urge; do not recommend / 飲尿後 *innyō go* after drinking urine / 必ず *kanarazu* always; without fail / うがいし *ugai shi* gargle / 二十分以上 *nijuppun ijō* for more than twenty minutes / 歯を磨く *ha o migaku* brush your teeth

動　飲尿しない ☞ 飲尿する *innyō suru* / 勧めない ☞ 勧める *susumeru* / うがいし ☞ うがいする *ugai suru*

注　The sentence-final こと indicates a strong command or prohibition. It is often used in signs: タバコを吸わないこと *tabako o suwanai koto* "No Smoking." / The pronunciation of 二十分 is discussed in 1m.

---

**8q**

かっこよく、優しく、お金持ちのO君は毎週末、高級レストランに誘ってくれる。

---

語　かっこよく handsome / 優しく *yasashiku* gentle; kind / お金持ち *o-kanemochi* rich / 毎週末 *mai-shūmatsu* every weekend / 高級レストラン *kōkyū resutoran* high-class restaurant / 誘ってくれる *sasotte kureru* invites (M-ko)

動　かっこよく ☞ かっこよい ☞ かっこうよい *kakkō yoi* / 優しく ☞ 優しい *yasashii* / 誘って ☞ 誘う *sasou*

注　Both かっこよく and 優しく are adverbial forms, which are used to link series of adjectives. Both of these words and お金持ちの modify O君. / かっこよい is a shortened form of かっこうよい, which means "having a nice, refined appearance" or, more colloquially, "good-looking" or "cool." It is also pronounced かっこいい or かっこういい.

---

**8r**

しかし、M子さんは憂鬱だ。

---

語　しかし however / 憂鬱だ *yūutsu da* is depressed; feels blue

注　This sentence echoes the story's title.

---

**8s**

「いま、飲んだワインが体内で温まり、彼は明日の朝また飲むんだわ」

語　いま now / 飲んだワイン *nonda wain* the wine he drank / 体内で *tainai de* inside his body / 温まり *atatamari* is becoming warmer / 彼 *kare* he / 明日の朝 *ashita no asa* tomorrow morning / また again / 飲む *nomu* will drink

注　The subject of 飲む is 彼, that is, Ｏ君.

**8t**

と想像するたびに、ご馳走がまずくなるからである。

語　と (quoting と) / 想像するたびに *sōzō suru tabi ni* every time she pictures in her mind (what she describes in 8s) / ご馳走 *go-chisō* gourmet food / まずくなる *mazuku naru* starts to taste bad / から because

動　まずく ☞ まずい

注　想像する *sōzō suru* means "to imagine; to picture in one's mind." / ご馳走 can mean food or drink to which one is treated, or it can refer to a luxurious meal. Here the focus is on the latter, as they are eating in an expensive restaurant where the food would normally be delicious. / The から explains why M-ko is depressed in 8r—she can no longer enjoy the delicious food because she keeps thinking about what will happen to the wine that her boyfriend is drinking.

# 9

初めて呼んだ
ホテトル嬢は隣の娘

*His First Call Girl Was
the Girl Next Door*

# 初めて呼んだ
# ホテトル嬢は隣の娘

オホーツク海に面した北海道Ａ町の助役Ｓさん（五九）は、六月初め、半年ぶりの東京出張に出かけた。いつもの出張の夜は、地元選出の代議士秘書に選挙区情勢の「取材」を受けるのだが、この日は秘書の日程が詰まっていた。

　東京の夜を一人で過ごせることになったＳさんは深夜、酔った頭で悩んだ。手には、Ａ町では見ることのない「ホテルに出張します」のピンクチラシがある。

「よし、証拠は残らない」

　と意を決したＳさんは、受話器を取り上げた。

　シャワーを浴び、酔いも少し冷めたところで、部屋のチャイムが鳴った。にこやかに、ゆっくりドアを開けたＳさんは目をむいた。女性はＳさんが住む公務員住宅の隣娘のＭ子ちゃんだったのだ。

# HIS FIRST CALL GIRL WAS THE GIRL NEXT DOOR

S (59) is deputy mayor of Town A on the Sea of Okhotsk in Hokkaido. At the beginning of June, he went on his first business trip to Tokyo in six months. Usually the evenings of his business trips are spent briefing his Diet representative's secretary on the latest goings-on in his district, but today the secretary's schedule was full.

Now S was able to spend the evening in Tokyo alone. Late that night, his brain foggy with drink, he tried to decide what to do. In his hand was something he had never seen in Town A: a flyer advertising a call girl service. "She'll come to your hotel," the ad said.

"Okay, no one will ever find out," he thought, and he picked up the telephone.

He had just taken a shower and sobered up a bit when the doorbell rang. Smiling, he slowly opened the door. But then his eyes widened. The woman was M-ko, the daughter of his neighbor back in the government employee housing complex where he lives in Town A.

「確か女子大の三年のはずだ。こんなとこで何をしているんだ」

　しかし、Ｓさんの叱咤にM子ちゃんはたじろがなかった。

「おじさんが呼んだんでしょ」

　旗色の悪くなったＳさんは、

「お父さんからの仕送りがあるはずだ。もっとまじめにやらなきゃだめじゃないか」

　と小一時間説教を続けたが、いかんせん迫力がない。M子ちゃんは冗談とも本気ともつかぬ口調でいった。

「延長する？」

　何もしなかったＳさんだが、延長なしで規定どおりの三万円を払った。M子ちゃんは、

「おばさんには内証にしといてあげるよ」

　と毅然とした顔で帰っていった。

　なぜ、いつから、きっかけは。何も聞き出せず、あまつさえ、しっぽをつかまれて帰郷したＳさんは、白髪が増えたような気がした。

"You're supposed to be a junior at a women's university. What are you doing in a place like this?"

M-ko was unfazed by S's scolding.

"You called for me, didn't you?" she replied.

That put S on the defensive.

"Your father must be sending you an allowance," he said. "Shouldn't you be behaving better?"

He lectured her for nearly an hour, but to no effect.

"You want to pay for some more time?" M-ko asked. He couldn't tell if she was joking or serious.

Though S had done nothing, he paid the 30,000 yen as agreed, with no extension.

"I won't tell your wife," M-ko said as she left, still with a stubborn expression.

Why? Since when? How did she get into this? Unable to find out anything from her and, even worse, caught in the act himself, S returned home, his head, it seemed to him, having grown even grayer.

**9a**

*Title:* 初めて呼んだホテトル嬢は隣の娘

語 初めて *hajimete* for the first time / 呼んだ *yonda* called / ホテトル嬢 *hotetoru jō* hotel call girl / 隣の娘 *tonari no musume* the neighbor's daughter

動 呼んだ ☞ 呼ぶ *yobu*

注 ホテトル is a blend of the words ホテル "hotel" and トルコ風呂 *Toruko-buro* "Turkish bath." A ホテトル嬢 is a prostitute who plies her trade at hotels. / The phrase 初めて呼んだホテトル嬢 indicates that this is the first time the protagonist of this story has hired a call girl.

文 The word トルコ風呂 formerly referred to bathhouses with private rooms where women would provide massages and sexual services to male customers. In the 1980s, after the Turkish government and others complained that genuine Turkish baths are not brothels, the bathhouse industry abandoned the term and coined the word ソープランド "soapland" to replace it. It is not known whether soap manufacturers have objected. / Although Japan enacted an antiprostitution law in 1956, the measure is inconsistently enforced and many forms of prostitution continue to be practiced openly.

**9b**

オホーツク海に面した北海道Ａ町の助役Ｓさん
（五九）は、六月初め、半年ぶりの東京出張
に出かけた。

語　オホーツク海 *Ohōtsuku Kai* Sea of Okhotsk / に面した
*ni men shita* facing onto / 北海道 *Hokkaidō* Hokkaido /
Ａ町 *Ē machi* Town A / 助役 *joyaku* deputy mayor / 六
月初め *rokugatsu hajime* at the beginning of June / 半年
ぶり *hantoshi-buri* for the first time in half a year / 東京
出張 *Tōkyō shutchō* business trip to Tokyo / 出かけた
*dekaketa* went; set out for

動　面した ☞ 面する *mensuru* / 出かけた ☞ 出かける
*dekakeru*

注　オホーツク海に面した and 北海道 both modify Ａ町,
so the phrase オホーツク海に面した北海道Ａ町 means
"Town A in Hokkaido, facing onto the Sea of Okhotsk."
/ 町 is the official designation for a local governmental
area smaller than a 市 *shi* "city" and larger than a 村
*mura* "village." The kanji 町 is read either *chō* or *machi*,
with some towns preferring one reading and other towns
the other. / Ａ助役 is a civil servant who serves as assis-
tant to the mayor of a city or town. / 半年ぶりの東京
出張 means "his first business trip to Tokyo in half a
year."

**9c**

いつもの出張の夜は、地元選出の代議士秘書に選挙区情勢の「取材」を受けるのだが、この日は秘書の日程が詰まっていた。

語　いつも always; usually / 出張 *shutchō* business trip / 夜 *yoru* evening; night / 地元 *jimoto* local / 選出 *senshutsu* elected / 代議士 *daigishi* Diet member / 秘書 *hisho* secretary / 選挙区 *senkyo-ku* electoral district / 情勢 *jōsei* situation / 取材 *shuzai* information-gathering / 受ける *ukeru* he receives / この日は *kono hi wa* on this day / 日程 *nittei* schedule / 詰まっていた *tsumatte ita* was full

動　詰まって ☞ 詰まる *tsumaru* / いた ☞ いる

注　いつもの出張の夜は means "Usually in the evening on his business trips." / Here the word 地元 refers to the location of a political power base, so 地元選出の代議士 means "a Diet member elected from S's district." / 代議士 usually refers to a member of the 衆議院 *Shūgiin* "House of Representatives," the lower and more powerful house in the Japanese Diet. / 取材 refers to gathering information for a particular purpose. 取材を受ける means roughly "to be interviewed." In this case, the Diet member's secretary would presumably ask S about the political situation in his boss's home district and perhaps put pressure on S to provide political support.

**9d**

東京の夜を一人で過ごせることになったＳさん
は深夜、酔った頭で悩んだ。

語　一人で *hitori de* by himself / 過ごせることになった
*sugoseru koto ni natta* became able to spend (the evening) /
深夜 *shin'ya* late at night / 酔った頭で *yotta atama de*
using his drunken brain / 悩んだ *nayanda* tried to decide
what to do

動　過ごせる ☞ 過ごす *sugosu* / なった ☞ なる / 酔った
☞ 酔う *you* / 悩んだ ☞ 悩む *nayamu*

注　The first half of this sentence means "S, who was now
able to spend the evening in Tokyo by himself." He
seems to have spent the evening getting drunk. / 悩む
here means "to be unable to make a decision."

**9e**

手には、Ａ町では見ることのない「ホテルに出張します」のピンクチラシがある。

語　手には *te ni wa* in his hand / 見ることのない *miru koto no nai* never seen (in Town A) / 「ホテルに出張します」 *hoteru ni shutchō shimasu* "We'll send (a woman) to your hotel." / ピンクチラシ advertising leaflet for a sex business

注　The word ピンク "pink" is a euphemism for sex-related matters. A ピンク映画 *pinku eiga* is a pornographic movie. / A チラシ is typically a one-page advertising flyer. The word is also written 散らし. / 手には modifies ある, the principal verb of this sentence. In other words, S was holding the leaflet in his hand. / The phrases 見ることのない and 「ホテルに出張します」の both modify ピンクチラシ.

文　A ピンクチラシ is typically a small printed notice advertising a call girl service, massage parlor, or other sex business. ピンクチラシ are often posted next to public telephones in nightlife areas or left in apartment building mailboxes.

**9f**

「よし、証拠は残らない」と意を決したＳさんは、受話器を取り上げた。

語　よし okay! here we go! / 証拠 *shōko* proof; evidence / 残

らない *nokoranai* will not remain / 意を決した *i o kesshita* decided / 受話器 *juwaki* telephone handset / 取り上げた *toriageta* picked up

動　残らない ☞ 残る *nokoru* / 決した ☞ 決する *kessuru* / 取り上げた ☞ 取り上げる *toriageru*

注　People say よし when they have decided to do or start something new or difficult. / The と before 意を決した Sさん is the quoting と, indicating what S said to himself when he decided to call the prostitution service.

---

**9g**

シャワーを浴び、酔いも少し冷めたところで、部屋のチャイムが鳴った。

---

語　シャワーを浴び *shawā o abi* he took a shower / 酔い *yoi* drunkenness / 少し *sukoshi* a little bit / 冷めた *sameta* lessened; cooled off / ところで when / 部屋のチャイム *heya no chaimu* doorbell / 鳴った *natta* rang

動　浴び ☞ 浴びる *abiru* / 冷めた ☞ 冷める *sameru* / 鳴った ☞ 鳴る *naru*

注　酔いが冷める means "to sober up." 冷める is an intransitive verb meaning "to cool off." In this context, it may also be written 覚める or 醒める.

## 9h

にこやかに、ゆっくりドアを開けたＳさんは目をむいた。

語 にこやかに with a smile / ゆっくり slowly / ドアを開けた *doa o aketa* opened the door / 目をむいた *me o muita* his eyes widened

動 開けた ☞ 開ける *akeru* / むいた ☞ 剥く *muku*

注 The idiom 目を剥く *me o muku* means "to open one's eyes in surprise or anger." The verb 剥く means "to peel," but 目を剥く has a different meaning from the English "to keep one's eyes peeled."

## 9i

女性はＳさんが住む公務員住宅の隣娘のＭ子ちゃんだったのだ。

語 女性 *josei* the woman / 住む *sumu* to live; to reside / 公務員 *kōmuin* civil servant / 住宅 *jūtaku* housing / 隣娘 *tonari musume* neighbor's daughter

注 公務員住宅 is a housing complex for public employees. Government agencies and private companies in Japan often provide low-cost housing for their employees. / The suffix ちゃん after Ｍ子 reflects both S's acquaintance with her and their difference in age. See also 6c. / The explanatory の in Ｍ子ちゃんだったのだ tells why S's eyes widened in 9h.

文　The words 女性, 女 *onna*, and 婦人 *fujin* all mean "woman." Of these, 女性 is the most neutral. In certain contexts, 女 *onna* might suggest "mistress" or "prostitute," while 婦人 *fujin* is avoided by some feminists and others for its old-fashioned, patronizing air. In many expressions, though, 女 and 婦人 are still the only choices, such as 女の子 *onna no ko* "girl" or 婦人科 *fujinka* "gynecology."

---

**9j**

「確<small>たし</small>か女子大<small>じょしだい</small>の三年<small>さんねん</small>のはずだ。こんなとこで何<small>なに</small>をしているんだ」

---

語　確か *tashika* I thought; I was pretty sure that / 女子大 *joshidai* women's university / 三年 *sannen* third year (student) / はずだ *hazu da* supposed to be / こんなとこで *konna toko de* in a place like this / 何をしているんだ *nani o shite iru n' da* what are you doing?

動　して ☞ する

注　The sentential adverb 確か indicates that the speaker is almost certain of what he saying, though the word does leave some room for doubt. Here it reinforces はず, which also indicates something that the speaker believes to be true. Thus 確か女子大の三年のはずだ means "I thought you were supposed to be a junior at a women's university." / 女子大 is an abbreviation for 女子大学 *joshi daigaku.* / とこ is an informal version of 所 *tokoro* "place." / The ん in しているんだ is a spoken form of the explanatory and nominalizing の.

---

**9k**

しかし、Ｓさんの叱咤にＭ子ちゃんはたじろがなかった。「おじさんが呼んだんでしょ」

語　しかし however / 叱咤 *shitta* scolding / たじろがなかった didn't flinch; was unfazed / おじさん (refers to older men) / 呼んだんでしょ *yonda n' desho* you called, didn't you

動　たじろがなかった ☞ たじろがない ☞ たじろぐ / 呼んだ ☞ 呼ぶ *yobu*

注　たじろぐ means "to be overcome; to be staggered." / The word おじさん is used to address or refer to men who are somewhat older than oneself. The word implies some degree of familiarity. The equivalent for referring to women is おばさん. The words おじいさん and おばあさん are used in the same way to refer to elderly men and women.

---

**9l**

旗色の悪くなったＳさんは、「お父さんからの仕送りがあるはずだ。もっとまじめにやらなきゃだめじゃないか」

語　旗色の悪くなった *hatairo no waruku natta* looked defeated / お父さん *otōsan* your father / 仕送り *shiokuri* allowance / もっとまじめに *motto majime ni* more seriously / やらなきゃだめじゃないか *yaranakya dame ja nai ka* aren't you supposed to behave?

---

**動** なった ☞ なる / やらなきゃ ☞ やらなければ ☞ やる / じゃない ☞ ではない *de wa nai*

**注** 旗色 literally means "the colors of flags." Originally, the idiom 旗色が悪い referred to an army's flags becoming less visible on the field of battle as the army is defeated. Here, it refers to the fact that S was in a weaker position to scold M-ko for working as a prostitute after she pointed out that he was the one who had hired her. / 仕送り is money sent periodically to help another person, such as a college student or an aged parent. / やらなきゃだめ is a contraction of やらなければだめ, which means "must do."

---

**9m**

と小一時間説教を続けたが、いかんせん迫力がない。

---

**語** 小一時間 *ko ichiji-kan* for nearly an hour / 説教を続けた *sekkyō o tsuzuketa* he continued preaching / いかんせん unfortunately / 迫力がない *hakuryoku ga nai* it had no effect (on her)

**動** 続けた ☞ 続ける *tsuzukeru* / ない ☞ ある

**注** The initial と in this sentence is the quoting と, referring to 9l. / Before expressions of quantity, the prefix 小 *ko* means "almost; slightly less than." / The original meaning of 説教 is "religious preaching; proselytizing." In its reference here to S's attempt to convince M-ko to quit prostitution, the word lacks any religious connotation. / 迫力 means "the ability to move or influence other people."

**9n**

M子ちゃんは冗談とも本気ともつかぬ口調でいった。「延長する？」

語　冗談 *jōdan* joke / 本気 *honki* honesty; seriousness / つかぬ unable to tell the difference / 口調 *kuchō* tone of voice / いった said / 延長する？ *enchō suru* do you want to extend the time?

動　つかぬ ☞ つく / いった ☞ 言う *iu, yū*

注　冗談とも本気ともつかぬ口調で means "in a tone of voice that S couldn't tell was joking or serious." / It seems that S had arranged to pay for one hour of M-ko's services. If he had agreed to the 延長, he would have had to pay an additional fee.

**9o**

何もしなかったSさんだが、延長なしで規定どおりの三万円を払った。

語　何もしなかった *nani mo shinakatta* had done nothing / 延長なしで *enchō nashi de* without an extension / 規定どおり *kitei dōri* as agreed / 三万円 *san man en* thirty thousand yen / 払った *haratta* he paid

動　しなかった ☞ しない ☞ する / 払った ☞ 払う *harau*

注　何もしなかった *nani mo shinakatta* refers to the fact that S had done nothing that he had paid the call girl for. / 規定 means "agreement; rules" and the suffix どおり,

also written 通り, means "in accordance with," so 規定通り means "as agreed."

---

**9p**

M子ちゃんは、「おばさんには内証にしといてあげるよ」と毅然とした顔で帰っていった。

---

**語** おばさん (refers to older women) / 内証にしといてあげる *naisho ni shitoite ageru* I'll keep it secret for you / 毅然とした *kizen to shita* stubborn / 顔 *kao* face; expression / 帰っていった *kaette itta* left

**動** しといて ☞ しておいて ☞ する, おく / した ☞ する / 帰って ☞ 帰る *kaeru* / いった ☞ 行く *iku*

**注** Here, おばさん refers to S's wife. M-ko uses this word because she is acquainted with S's wife. If M-ko had never met S's wife or was not on familiar terms with her, she would have used the word 奥さん *okusan* "wife" instead. / 内証 means "secret; confidential." 内証にする means "to keep confidential." / あげる indicates that M-ko will keep the secret as a favor to S.

**9q**

なぜ、いつから、きっかけは。何も聞き出せず、あまつさえ、しっぽをつかまれて帰郷したＳさんは、白髪が増えたような気がした。

語　なぜ why? / いつから since when? / きっかけは *kikkake wa* how did she get into this? / 何も *nani mo* nothing / 聞き出せず *kikidasezu* unable to ask / あまつさえ in addition; even more so / しっぽをつかまれて sheepishly; having been caught in an act of weakness / 帰郷した *kikyō shita* returned to his home town / 白髪 *shiraga* white hair; gray hair / 増えたような気がした *fueta yō na ki ga shita* seemed (to him) to have increased

動　聞き出せず ☞ 聞き出せる ☞ 聞き出す *kikidasu* / つかまれて ☞ つかまれる ☞ つかむ / 帰郷した ☞ 帰郷する *kikyō suru* / 増えた ☞ 増える *fueru* / した ☞ する

注　The first sentence consists of the questions that S wanted to ask M-ko but couldn't: Why and when had she started working as a call girl? What led her to do it? / きっかけ means "cause; reason; start." / 聞き出す means "to ask." It often refers to an attempt to extract information from someone who is reluctant to reveal it. / The idiom しっぽをつかむ means "to reveal a person's weaknesses or secrets." The literal meaning is "to grab by the tail."

## AUTHOR'S PROFILE

TOM GALLY—writer, lexicographer, and translator—received master's degrees in linguistics and mathematics from the University of Chicago. He is the author of *Handy Japanese: The Basics in 50 Easy Lessons* and *English for Scientists*, and general editor of *Kenkyusha's Guide to Quantitative Expressions in English*. His dictionary work includes *Kenkyusha's New Japanese-English Dictionary, 5th Edition*, as well as its online version as part of the Kenkyusha Online Dictionary. Among his translated works are *Japanese Verbs at a Glance*, *Amazing Science Tricks for Kids and Parents*, and *Jazz Up Your Japanese with Onomatopoeia: For All Levels*. He is presently associate professor in the College of Arts and Sciences at the University of Tokyo.

9 784990 284817